The Top 100 Recipes from Food and Drink

Digital food photography by Steve Lee

This book is based on the television series entitled Food and Drink,
produced for BBC Television by Endemol UK Productions.
Executive Producer for series 13 and 14: Tim Hincks
Executive Producer for series 15: Gloria Wood
Series Producer for series 13 and 14: Gloria Wood
Series Producer for series 15: Lyndsay Davis

Published by BBC Wordwide Ltd
80 Wood Lane
London W12 0TT

First published 2002
Reprinted 2002 (twice)
© Antony Worrall Thompson and Endemol UK PLC 2002
The moral right of the author has been asserted.

Food photography by Steve Lee © BBC Worldwide 2002

ISBN: 0 563 48844 1

Recipe Development: Orla Broderick

Commissioning Editor: Vivien Bowler
Project Editors: Rachel Copus and Rhianwen Bailey
Copy-editor: Ruth Baldwin
Cover Art Director: Pene Parker
Book Designer/Photo Art Director: Lisa Pettibone
Home Economist: Lorna Brash
Stylist: Lucy Pearse

Set in Caecilia and Foundry Sans
Printed and bound in France by Imprimerie Pollina s.a. - L88271
Colour separations by Kestrel Digital Colour, Chelmsford

For more information about this and other BBC Books, please visit our
website on www. bbcshop.com

The Top 100 Recipes from
Food and Drink

Antony Worrall Thompson

Contents

Introduction

I still feel like a new boy on *Food and Drink* even though I have been chief presenter for over five years. It was always an ambition of mine to present *Food and Drink*, the godmother of all TV cookery shows and I was over the moon when I was offered the position.

And so it gives me pleasure to present to you my first *Food and Drink* cookbook, combining the best dishes of the last few series – *The Top Ten Best-of-British Dishes*, *The Top Ten Classic Dishes* and *The Top Ten Holiday Dishes*, together with other fabulous 'quickies' that will inspire you to get into that kitchen.

None of the dishes is beyond reach, it has always been a policy of *Food and Drink* not to cook complicated dishes. This is food you'll very much want to eat rather than just admire. Most of the dishes you'll recognize as old favourites, but interestingly many of them are back in vogue as the public starts to reject outlandish and over-complicated food.

A recent survey discovered the British mouth waters much more at the expectation of a good old roast dinner than at the sound of some overworked 'fusion' dish. That's great news, as in this book you'll find the ultimate roast rib of beef, and wonderful roast pork with fail-safe crackling.

I have really enjoyed filming *Food and Drink* with the fantastic help of all at Endemol UK including Peter Bazalgette, Tim Hinks, Linda Clifford and of course Jane Root at the BBC, who has commissioned *Food and Drink* for the last twenty-one years. My thanks would not be complete without mentioning my old mate Oz Clarke and of course Chris Kelly and Jilly Goolden from earlier series and my co-food presenter Emma Crowhurst. I have worked with some great directors, producers, cameramen, sound and lighting engineers but special thanks must go to all the runners who do so much behind the scenes, and keep my house – where we film the series – clean and tidy, without getting much credit.

Also, where would I be without the home economists who make my life easy, check recipes, work them out to the letter and back up my very move, so thank-you Anna-Lisa Aldridge, who worked with me on the last three series and Orla Broderick, chief honcho in the home-economist world, who tried, tested and tested again with Anna-Lisa all the recipes in this book.

Finally, thank-you, the public, who continue to support *Food and Drink* year on year … happy cooking.

Antony Worrall Thompson

The Top Ten
Best-of-British Dishes

For sheer comfort value, nothing can beat good British food, cooked well. The viewers of *Food and Drink* chose these top ten British dishes – recipes that will prove to be winners on anyone's table, at any time of the year.

1 Steak and Kidney Pudding page 28

2 Lancashire Hotpot page 50

3 Beef in Stout with Dumplings page 26

4 Faggots with Onion Gravy page 64

5 Bacon and Pease Pudding page 56

6 Bread-and-Butter Pudding page 124

7 Toad in the Hole page 66

8 Treacle Sponge page 132

9 Roast Loin of Pork with Apple Sauce page 60

10 Rack of Lamb with a Pistachio Crust page 48

The Top Ten
Classic Dishes

However adventurous your cooking may be, there are certain dishes that will guarantee you success time and time again. Here are the top ten such classics, as voted for by the viewers of *Food and Drink*.

The Top Ten
Holiday Dishes

Have you ever wished you could recreate that Paella you ate in the shade of an olive tree in Seville? This selection of holiday favourites, voted by the viewers of *Food and Drink*, will transport you back to those lazy, pleasure-filled days.

The Top Ten

1 Pear, Roquefort and Croûton Salad

SERVES 4

20-cm/8-in piece French baguette (slightly stale is best)

50 g/2 oz Roquefort cheese, crumbled

75 g/3 oz ricotta cheese

50 g/2 oz unsalted butter, at room temperature

1 tbsp snipped fresh chives

1 tsp lemon juice

2 Conference pears (ripe but firm)

100 g/4 oz bag garden salad with watercress

25 g/1 oz walnuts (lightly toasted or very fresh), coarsely chopped

1 1/2 tsp balsamic vinegar

2 tbsp extra-virgin olive oil

salt and freshly ground black pepper

Very stylish, very simple and very delicious: the perfect starter! There is now a wide variety of mixed salad bags in every major supermarket and I'm sure we all have our own favourites. However, a garden salad with watercress, with its peppery bite, works particularly well in this dish. The combination is classic, but feel free to substitute Gorgonzola, Stilton or Fourme d'Ambert for the Roquefort.

1 Preheat the oven to 150°C/300°F/Gas 2; fan oven 130°C from cold. Cut the baguette on the diagonal into twelve very thin slices, discarding the ends. Arrange on a baking sheet and cook in the oven for 15–20 minutes until crisp and lightly golden.

2 Meanwhile, place the Roquefort in a bowl with the ricotta, butter, chives and lemon juice. Mash together with a fork until well blended and season generously with pepper.

3 Peel the pears, then remove the cores and cut the flesh into slices that will fit nicely on to the croûtons. Spread the toasted croûtons thickly with the Roquefort mixture and then arrange the pear slices in an overlapping layer on top.

4 Place the salad leaves in a large bowl with the walnuts and sprinkle over the vinegar. Season generously and lightly dress with the oil. Divide the salad leaves into wide-rimmed bowls and arrange three of the croûtons on top of each one. Serve at once.

2 Caesar Salad

SERVES 4–6

2 egg yolks (preferably free-range or organic)

1 tbsp red wine vinegar

1 tbsp lemon juice

5 canned anchovy fillets, drained and mashed to a paste

1 tsp anchovy essence

3 garlic cloves, crushed

1 tbsp Dijon mustard

$1/2$ tsp English mustard powder

2 tsp Worcestershire sauce

300 ml/$1/2$ pint olive oil (good-quality)

2 large Cos lettuces or 6 Little Gem lettuces, separated into leaves

75 g/3 oz freshly grated Parmesan cheese

FOR THE PARMESAN CROÛTONS:

175 g/6 oz country-style bread, crusts removed and cut into 1-cm/$1/2$-in cubes

3 tbsp olive oil

25 g/1 oz freshly grated Parmesan cheese

salt and freshly ground pepper

There are those who insist that anchovies are wrong in a Caesar salad. However, I think they are vital, but don't faff around with marinated anchovies or shards of Parmesan – a well-made Caesar salad does not need unnecessary adornment. Traditionally the dressing would be made with a 1-minute coddled or boiled egg yolk, but perhaps life is too short to be that pernickety. When buying eggs look out for the Lion Quality Mark which guarantees salmonella-free eggs.

1 Preheat the oven to 150°C/300°F/Gas 2; fan oven 130°C from cold. To make the Parmesan croûtons, place the bread cubes in a baking dish and drizzle over the oil, then season generously. Toss until well combined and bake for 20 minutes, then remove from the oven and scatter over the Parmesan. Return to the oven and bake for another 20–25 minutes until crisp and golden brown, stirring occasionally. These can be made in advance and stored in an airtight container.

2 To make the dressing, place the egg yolks in a food processor with the vinegar, lemon juice, anchovy fillets, anchovy essence, garlic, Dijon mustard, mustard powder, Worcestershire sauce and enough pepper to suit your taste – 1-1$1/2$ teaspoons is about right. Blend together until well combined, then with the machine running pour the oil in a slow trickle through the feeder tube. Transfer to a jug and chill until needed. Bring back to room temperature before using and season to taste.

3 To prepare the salad, tear the lettuces into bite-sized pieces and place in a large bowl. Add enough of the dressing just to coat (not drown) the leaves, then fold in the Parmesan. Toss to combine, transfer to wide-rimmed bowls, scatter over the Parmesan croûtons and serve at once.

3 Salade Niçoise

HOLIDAY DISHES

SERVES 4

4 x 100 g/4 oz fresh tuna steaks, each 2.5 cm/1 in thick

12 new salad potatoes

4 eggs (preferably free-range or organic), at room temperature

100 g/4 oz extra-fine French beans, trimmed

4 Little Gem lettuce hearts, quartered lengthways and separated into leaves

4 ripe plum tomatoes, roughly chopped

1 red onion, finely sliced

6 canned anchovy fillets, drained and cut lengthways into thin strips

16 pitted black olives in brine, drained

8 fresh basil leaves, torn

FOR THE MARINADE:

7 tbsp extra-virgin olive oil

3 tbsp aged red wine vinegar

2 tbsp chopped fresh flatleaf parsley

2 tbsp snipped fresh chives

2 garlic cloves, finely chopped

salt and freshly ground black pepper

A deliciously informal dish that can be made as generous as you wish, depending on the amount of vegetables. The tuna is cooked medium rare so that it remains moist, but cook it for a minute or two longer if you prefer, or just use canned tuna. Serve this Provençal favourite with a well-chilled, high-acidity wine to do justice to the strong flavours. The classic match would be a dry white from Provence (Bellet or Palette) which should be available from most good off-licences.

1 To make the marinade, place the oil, vinegar, parsley, chives, garlic and a teaspoon each of salt and pepper in a bowl and whisk to combine.

2 Place the tuna in a shallow, non-metallic dish and pour over half of the marinade. Cover with plastic film and chill for 1–2 hours to allow the flavours to penetrate the tuna, turning every 30 minutes or so.

3 Place the potatoes in a pan of boiling salted water, cover and simmer for 15–18 minutes until just tender. Drain and leave to cool completely, then cut into quarters lengthways.

4 Place the eggs in a small pan and just cover with boiling water, then cook for 6 minutes. Drain and rinse under cold running water, then remove the shells and cut each egg in half. Plunge the French beans in a pan of boiling salted water and blanch for a minute or so, then drain and refresh under cold running water.

5 Heat a griddle pan for 5 minutes. Remove the tuna from the marinade, shaking off any excess. Cook the tuna steaks for 2–3 minutes on each side, depending on how rare you like your fish.

6 Arrange the lettuce leaves on serving plates or one large platter and add the potatoes, French beans, tomatoes, onion and anchovies. Place the tuna steaks on top and drizzle over the remaining marinade. Scatter over the eggs, olives and torn basil leaves to serve.

4 Crab and Asparagus Fettuccine

SERVES 6

2 tbsp extra-virgin olive oil

1 shallot, finely diced

1 tsp fresh soft thyme leaves

2 tsp anchovy essence

150 ml/^{1}/$_4$ pint dry white wine

150 ml/^{1}/$_4$ pint fresh fish stock (from a carton is fine)

450 g/1 lb asparagus, trimmed and cut into 4-cm/1^1/$_2$-in pieces

350 g/12 oz white crab meat, thawed if frozen

750 g/1^1/$_2$ lb fresh or 350 g/12 oz dried fettuccine

50 g/2 oz unsalted butter

juice of ^{1}/$_2$ lemon

2 heaped tbsp chopped fresh flatleaf parsley

salt and freshly ground black pepper

Flavour-packed, the crab adds a wonderful zap to this fresh pasta dish. It works well as a starter or is perfect for a quick supper on a cold winter's night. Adding the browned butter at the end may sound fattening, and you'd be correct, but it is essential for that touch of magic. Making your own fish stock is really very easy. Simply simmer some white- or flat-fish bones with a good splash of dry white wine, a squeeze of lemon juice, a roughly chopped shallot, a bouquet garni and a few white peppercorns for no more than 20 minutes, then strain and reduce to taste. Alternatively, there are now some very good fresh fish stocks sold in supermarkets.

1 Heat the oil in a large, heavy-based frying pan, add the shallot and cook gently for about 5 minutes until softened but not coloured. Stir in the thyme with the anchovy essence, wine and fish stock and bring to the boil, then simmer until the liquid has reduced by half. Keep warm.

2 Meanwhile, bring a large pan of salted water to the boil. Add the asparagus and cook for 3–4 minutes until just tender. Drain the asparagus and refresh under cold running water, reserving the cooking liquid and returning it to the pan. Stir the asparagus and the crab into the reduced shallot liquid.

3 Return the reserved asparagus cooking liquid to the boil. Tip in the fettuccine and, depending on the manufacturer's instructions, cook for about 2–3 minutes for fresh or 8–12 minutes for dried. Drain, quickly refresh under cold running water and stir into the crab sauce.

4 Melt the butter in a frying pan and cook until nutty and golden but not burnt, squeeze in the lemon juice and add the parsley, swirling to combine. Pour over the fettuccine and crab mixture and toss gently to combine. Season to taste and serve at once in wide-rimmed bowls.

5 Warm Chicken Liver Salad

SERVES 4–6

450 g/1 lb baby new potatoes

3 tbsp extra-virgin olive oil

75 g/3 oz unsalted butter

1 onion, finely chopped

1/4 tsp dried red chilli flakes

1/2 tsp chopped fresh thyme leaves

2 tbsp white wine vinegar

4 large eggs (preferably free-range or organic)

225 g/8 oz black pudding, cut into 1-cm/1/2-in slices

350 g/12 oz fresh chicken livers, trimmed and cut into 1-cm/1/2-in slices

1 tbsp balsamic vinegar

4 tbsp red wine

175 g/6 oz mixed greens, such as baby spinach or rocket

salt and freshly ground black pepper

I just love this simple salad. Chicken livers are so cheap – buy the freshest you can find, preferably free-range or even better organic, but remove any green stains before using them. Each portion of salad is served with a poached egg on top – these are so easy to prepare in advance, then you just slip them back into hot salted water when you are ready to serve.

1 Place the potatoes in a pan of boiling salted water, cover and simmer for 10–12 minutes until tender. Drain and leave to cool until warm, then cut each one in half.

2 Heat 1 tablespoon of the oil with a knob of butter in a wok or frying pan and fry the onion for 5 minutes until softened. Stir in the chilli flakes and thyme, then add the potatoes and cook for 8–10 minutes until the potatoes are crispy and golden brown, tossing occasionally.

3 Heat 2.25 litres/4 pints water in a large pan. Add the white wine vinegar and bring to the boil. When the water is bubbling, break the eggs one-by-one into the water, then move the pan to the edge of the heat and simmer gently for 3 minutes. Remove each egg with a slotted spoon and plunge into a bowl of iced water. When cold, trim down any ragged ends from the cooked egg white.

4 Heat another tablespoon of the oil with a knob of butter in a large frying pan. Add the black pudding and fry for a minute on each side until just tender. Transfer to a plate and keep warm. Add the remaining oil and 25 g/1 oz of the butter to the pan. Season the chicken livers and add to the pan, then fry for 3–4 minutes, turning once, until sizzling and golden brown but still pink in the middle. Add to the plate with the black pudding.

5 Deglaze the pan with the balsamic vinegar, scraping the bottom with a wooden spoon to remove any sediment. Pour in the wine, boil to reduce a little and then fold in the rest of the butter.

6 Add the poached eggs to a pan of boiling salted water and heat through for 1–2 minutes. Add the greens to the potatoes and toss until they are just beginning to wilt. Season, divide among four serving plates and arrange the chicken livers, black pudding and poached eggs on top. Spoon on the balsamic dressing to serve.

6 Gravadlax with Sweet Mustard and Dill Sauce

No. 10 HOLIDAY DISHES

SERVES UP TO 20

100 g/4 oz coarse rock salt

75 g/3 oz caster sugar

1 tbsp white peppercorns, crushed

2 large bunches fresh dill, finely chopped

2 x 900 g/2 lb thick salmon fillets, skin on, scaled and pin bones removed

rye bread, to serve

FOR THE MUSTARD AND DILL SAUCE:

2 tbsp Dijon mustard

1 tbsp caster sugar

1 tbsp white wine vinegar

1 egg yolk (preferably free-range or organic)

150 ml/¼ pint groundnut or vegetable oil

1 tbsp chopped fresh dill

salt and freshly ground black pepper

The Scandinavian alternative to smoked salmon. The best cut for this dish is the middle of the fish. Ask your fishmonger to cut the salmon in half lengthways, then scale it and remove all the bones. Salmon is very cheap nowadays because the majority is farmed, so don't worry about the large quantity needed for this recipe. Farmed salmon is a good product, but think of it as you would haddock: no longer an indulgence (such as wild salmon), more a way of life!

1 To make the curing mixture, place the salt, sugar and crushed white pepper-corns in a bowl. Add half of the dill and stir to combine.

2 Use plastic film to line a large, shallow, rectangular dish which fits the salmon comfortably. Sprinkle a quarter of the curing mixture over the base of the dish and lay one of the salmon fillets on top, skin-side down. Sprinkle half of the curing mixture on top and cover with the other salmon fillet, skin-side up. Sprinkle the remaining curing mixture on top and wrap the salmon in the cling film.

3 Weigh the salmon down with some weights or cans to help remove any excess liquid or moisture. Place in the fridge for 2–3 days, turning the salmon over every 6 hours or so.

4 Rinse the cure off the gravadlax and pat dry with kitchen paper. Lay a large piece of cling film on the work surface and place one of the salmon fillets on top, skin-side down. Cover with the remaining dill and place the other salmon fillet on top, skin-side up. Wrap tightly in the cling film and chill for another 6 hours.

5 To make the sauce, place the mustard, sugar, vinegar and egg yolk in a large bowl and whisk to combine. Add the oil drop by drop to begin with, then in a steady stream, whisking constantly, until the sauce becomes thick and smooth. Stir in the dill and season to taste.

6 To serve, cut the gravadlax into thin slices, leaving the skin behind (gravadlax is traditionally served thicker than smoked salmon). Place three or four slices on each serving plate and add a spoonful of the sauce to the side. Serve at once with the rye bread.

7 Roasted Red Pepper Soup

SERVES 6–8

6 red peppers

2 tbsp olive oil

2 onions, finely chopped

1 tbsp fennel seeds

1 tsp fresh soft thyme leaves

225 g/8 oz plum tomatoes, peeled, seeded and diced

1 tbsp tomato purée

1.5 litres/2$1/2$ pints vegetable or chicken stock

300 ml/1$1/2$ pints double cream

2 tbsp shredded fresh basil

Maldon sea salt and freshly ground black pepper

crème fraîche and *Parmesan Croutons* (p. 11), to garnish (optional)

A rich and robust soup that makes a great starter at any time of the year, or a satisfying lunch or light supper. If you are watching your weight like me, you can omit the cream and use half the olive oil stated in the recipe with perfectly good results. You might just need to add a little more stock or water to thin the soup down after blending. I like to serve it with a spoonful of crème fraîche and some crunchy Parmesan croûtons, but of course these are optional extras.

1 Preheat the grill. Arrange the red peppers on the grill rack and cook for 20–30 minutes until well charred and blistered, turning regularly. Transfer to a polythene bag, and secure in a knot. Leave the peppers to cool completely, then peel. Chop the flesh, reserving any juices and discarding the seeds.

2 Heat the oil in a large pan. Add the onions, fennel seeds and thyme and cook for about 5 minutes until the onions are softened but not coloured, stirring occasionally. Add the peppers and any reserved juices with the tomatoes, tomato purée and stock. Bring to the boil, reduce the heat and simmer for 15 minutes until the mixture has thickened and reduced slightly.

3 Place the soup in a food processor in small batches or blitz with a hand-held blender, then pass through a fine sieve if you like a really smooth finish. Pour back into a clean pan and stir in the cream and basil. Season to taste and just warm through. Ladle into bowls and garnish with the crème fraîche and *Parmesan Croûtons*, if liked.

8 Pumpkin and Bean Soup with Parsley Purée

SERVES 10–12

300 g/11 oz dried white beans, soaked overnight

2 tbsp finely chopped fresh sage

4 garlic cloves, finely chopped

2 fresh bay leaves

2 fresh thyme sprigs

2 kg/4$^{1}/_{2}$ lb wedge pumpkin or butternut squash

3 tbsp olive oil

2 onions, finely chopped

2 carrots, finely chopped

2 celery sticks, finely chopped

2.25 litres/4 pints vegetable or chicken stock

Maldon sea salt and freshly ground black pepper

rustic bread, to serve

FOR THE PARSLEY PURÉE:

2 garlic cloves, peeled

15 g/$^{1}/_{2}$ oz fresh flatleaf parsley, stalks discarded

4 tbsp freshly grated Parmesan cheese

4 tbsp extra-virgin olive oil

$^{1}/_{2}$ lemon, pips removed

Pumpkin and beans are a surprisingly good partnership, a lovely winter warmer. As this soup makes such a large quantity you may want to freeze some of it. Simply pour into freezer bags or lidded containers – leaving space to allow for expansion. Haricot or cannellini beans work best in this recipe: just use the freshest you can find or they can take an age to cook.

1 Place the beans in a pan with plenty of water and boil fast for 15 minutes. Drain, rinse and return to the pan, then cover with 2.5 cm/1 in of fresh water. Add half of the sage and garlic, the bay leaves and thyme and bring to the boil, then reduce the heat and simmer for 1 hour or until the beans are tender, topping up with boiling water as necessary. Drain and rinse briefly.

2 Preheat the oven to 240°C/475°F/Gas 9; fan oven 210°C from cold. Cut the pumpkin or squash into wedges, not more than 7.5 cm/3 in thick, and scoop out the seeds using a large spoon. Brush the wedges all over using 1 tablespoon of the oil and place them in a roasting tin. Season generously and roast on a high shelf in the oven for about 45 minutes until softened and caramelized, turning once.

3 Heat the remaining oil in a large pan. Add the remaining sage and garlic, the onions, carrots and celery and cook for 10–15 minutes until softened but not browned, stirring occasionally. Pour in the stock and bring to the boil, season and simmer for 20 minutes until the vegetables are completely tender.

4 Leave the pumpkin to cool, then scoop the flesh away from the skin: you should have about 1 kg/2$^{1}/_{4}$ lb. Discard the skin. Add the flesh to the pan and simmer for another 15–20 minutes until the pumpkin is tender and has started to collapse. Whizz the soup to a purée with a hand blender or in batches in a food processor, then add the beans, season to taste and reheat gently.

5 Meanwhile, make the parsley purée. Place the garlic, parsley and Parmesan in a mini blender with $^{1}/_{2}$ teaspoon salt and whizz to a purée. Add the oil and a squeeze of lemon juice, then blend again briefly to combine. Season to taste and transfer to a small serving bowl. Cover with cling film and chill until ready to serve. To serve, ladle the soup into bowls and top each serving with a teaspoonful of the parsley purée. Serve hot with the bread.

9 Jerusalem Artichoke Soup with Crispy Bacon

SERVES 6

1 tbsp olive oil

175 g/6 oz smoked streaky bacon lardons

450 g/1 lb Jerusalem artichokes, peeled, diced and submerged in water with a dash of lemon juice

1 onion, diced

225 g/8 oz floury potatoes, diced

2 garlic cloves, finely chopped

1 celery stick, diced

100 g/4 oz unsalted butter

1 heaped tsp fresh soft thyme leaves

1 litre/1³/₄ pints chicken or vegetable stock

300 ml/¹/₂ pint double cream or milk

pinch freshly grated nutmeg

50 g/2 oz tender young spinach leaves

salt and freshly ground black pepper

This recipe is adapted from Jane Grigson's wonderful Palestine soup, first published in *English Food*. However, I have made some changes to the basic recipe with some very pleasing results, if I say so myself! When buying Jerusalem artichokes, choose the smoothest, most evenly sized specimens. The knobblier they are, the harder they are to peel and the more peelings you end up with – so always buy more than the recipe states to allow for that extra waste.

1 Heat a large, heavy-based pan with a lid. Add the oil, tip in the bacon and cook over a medium heat for 8–10 minutes, stirring occasionally, until it releases some of its fat and becomes crispy and golden. Remove from the pan with a slotted spoon, leaving the fat behind, and set aside on kitchen paper to drain.

2 Drain the artichokes and add them to the bacon fat in the pan, stirring to coat. Add the onion, potatoes, garlic, celery, half the butter and the thyme, then stir to combine until the butter has melted. Cover and cook for 10 minutes, shaking the pan occasionally, until the potatoes have started to soften but not colour.

3 Pour the stock into the pan, bring to the boil, then reduce to a simmer and cook for another 10 minutes or so until all the vegetables have softened and are completely tender. Leave to cool a little and blend with a hand-held mixer or in a food processor in batches until smooth. If you would like a squeaky-smooth soup, pass it through a fine sieve. Return the soup to the pan.

4 Add the cream or milk to the soup with the remaining butter, the nutmeg and spinach and reheat gently, stirring until the spinach has wilted. Season to taste and ladle into warmed soup bowls. Scatter the reserved crispy bacon on top and serve at once.

10 Seared Salmon with Sweet Pea Guacamole

SERVES 4

about 4 tbsp extra-virgin olive oil

4 x 100 g/4 oz salmon fillets, skin on, scaled and pin bones removed

375 g/12 oz frozen peas

juice of 1 lime

2 tbsp fresh coriander leaves, plus extra to garnish

2 red bird's eye chillies, seeded and diced

$1/2$ tsp ground cumin

$1/2$ tsp ground coriander

good pinch ground paprika, plus extra to garnish

8 sun blush tomatoes in oil, drained and finely chopped, or 2 plum tomatoes, peeled, seeded and diced

1 small red onion, finely diced

about 4 tbsp soured cream

salt and freshly ground black pepper

This sweet pea guacamole is an interesting dish that I first produced on the BBC's *Ready Steady Cook* when confronted with a bag of frozen peas. To me frozen peas are something of a miracle. The guacamole is extremely versatile and can be used as a dip with tortilla or corn chips, or as an accompaniment to a bowl of chilli con carne. I also like it stirred into some freshly cooked tagliatelle, perhaps with a spoonful or two of soured cream.

1 Place the peas in a pan of boiling salted water and cook for 4–5 minutes until just tender. Drain, refresh under cold running water and set aside. Blend together the remaining oil, the lime juice, fresh coriander and chillies in a food processor until reasonably smooth.

2 Heat a heavy-based frying pan and pour in enough oil for a thin coating on the base – 1 tablespoon should be more than enough. Season the salmon fillets and place them in the pan, skin-side down. Cook for 2–3 minutes over a high heat, then turn over, reduce the heat slightly and cook for another minute or so until just tender. Remove from the heat.

3 Add the cooked peas to the food processor with the ground cumin, ground coriander, paprika, 1 teaspoon salt and $1/2$ teaspoon pepper and blend again until smooth (don't worry if there are a few lumps). Tip the pea mixture into a bowl and fold in the sun-dried tomatoes or tomato dice and red onion. Season to taste and arrange small mounds on serving plates with a dollop of soured cream on top and a salmon fillet to the side. Garnish with a sprinkling of paprika and some coriander leaves before serving.

11 Boeuf Bourguignonne

4 tbsp olive oil

1 large carrot, cut into chunks

1 large onion, cut into chunks

2 celery sticks, roughly chopped

2 bottles red Burgundy wine

2 fresh thyme sprigs

1 head garlic, cut in half horizontally

4 fresh bay leaves

1.5 kg/3 lb chuck or blade beef steak, cut into 5-cm/2-in pieces

50 g/2 oz unsalted butter

225 g/8 oz smoked streaky bacon or pancetta, cut into lardons

450 g/1 lb shallots, peeled

2 tbsp plain flour

300 ml/¹/₂ pint fresh beef stock (from a carton is fine)

350 g/12 oz small chestnut mushrooms, trimmed

5 tbsp brandy

salt and freshly ground black pepper

chopped fresh flatleaf parsley, to garnish

steamed purple sprouting broccoli and *Dijon Mash* (p. 110), to serve

This classic French casserole is one of the truly great dishes of the world. It is as delicious to eat as it is easy to prepare – the beef literally melts in the mouth. If you'd like to thicken the sauce before serving, simply strain the liquid into a large pan and bring to the boil, covering the casserole with a lid to keep it warm. Reduce the heat and simmer the sauce until it has reached the desired consistency, then pour it back over the casserole, warm through and serve.

1 Heat 1 tablespoon of the oil in a large pan. Add the carrot, onion and celery and cook for 2–3 minutes, stirring occasionally. Pour in the wine and stir in the thyme, garlic and two of the bay leaves. Bring to the boil, then reduce the heat and simmer for 15 minutes. Allow to cool completely.

2 Place the beef in a large, non-metallic bowl and pour over the wine mixture. Cover with cling film and place in the fridge overnight to marinate.

3 Preheat the oven to 150°C/300°F/Gas 2; fan oven 130°C from cold. Strain the beef into a colander set over a bowl. Reserve the marinade and set aside.

4 Heat 25 g/1 oz of the butter and another tablespoon of the oil in a large frying pan. Add the bacon or pancetta and cook until sizzling and golden brown, stirring occasionally. Stir in the shallots, cook until brown and then transfer to a large, flameproof casserole dish.

5 Heat another tablespoon of the oil in the frying pan. Pat dry the drained beef cubes with kitchen paper. Add half of the beef to the pan and cook until browned on all sides.

6 Remove the beef from the pan with a slotted spoon and add to the bacon and shallot mixture in the casserole dish. Repeat with the remaining beef.

contd. overleaf

7 Add two to three large spoonfuls of the reserved marinade mixture to the pan and allow to bubble down, scraping the bottom of the pan with a wooden spoon to remove any sediment. Pour into the casserole dish.

8 Sprinkle the flour into the casserole dish and then add the remaining marinade mixture, bay leaves and the beef stock, stirring to combine. Season generously and bring to the boil, then cover and place in the oven for 3–3^1/$_2$ hours until the beef is very tender but still holding its shape.

9 Half-way through cooking, heat the remaining oil and butter in a large frying pan and cook the mushrooms until just tender and lightly browned, stirring. Add the brandy and cook for another few minutes, then stir into the casserole dish and return to the oven for the remaining cooking time.

10 Remove the casserole from the oven and season to taste. Sprinkle lavishly with the parsley and serve directly from the casserole with bowls of steamed purple sprouting broccoli and *Dijon Mash*.

12 Pepper Steak

SERVES 2

1 tbsp white peppercorns

1 tbsp black peppercorns

450 g/1 lb piece sirloin or rump steak, about 4 cm/1¹/₂ in thick

2 tsp groundnut oil

50 g/2 oz unsalted butter

2 shallots, finely chopped

85 ml/3 fl oz fresh beef stock (from a carton is fine)

2 tsp Worcestershire sauce

2 tsp Dijon mustard

3 tbsp double cream

1–2 tsp drained green peppercorns in brine, rinsed

2 tbsp brandy

salt

chips and watercress salad, to serve

I could have called this steak au poivre, but I try to avoid mixing languages, and anyway the French classic doesn't use quite the same ingredients. Dishes come and go as food fashions are affected by prevailing whims. 'Real' food, such as this dish, sticks around forever. For me the occasional piece of red meat in a rich, creamy sauce served with chips and a refreshing watercress salad is delicious. Remember my motto: 'Everything in moderation, and a little in excess'.

1 Lightly crush the white and black peppercorns using a pestle and mortar, then tip on to a flat plate. Pat the steak dry with kitchen paper and press the crushed peppercorns on to both sides, using your hands. If you have time, cover with foil or cling film and leave at room temperature for 2–3 hours to allow the flavours to infuse.

2 Heat the oil in a heavy-based frying pan over a high heat. Add the steak and cook for 2 minutes on each side, then reduce the heat, add half the butter and continue to cook the steak for 5–10 minutes, turning once, depending on how rare you like it. Transfer the steak to a plate, season to taste with salt and set aside in a warm place to rest while you make the sauce.

3 Pour away any excess fat from the pan, add the remaining butter and fry the shallots for a few minutes until softened but not browned. Add the stock and Worcestershire sauce and cook rapidly, scraping the bottom of the pan with a wooden spoon to release any sediment. Stir in the mustard, cream and green peppercorns, then season to taste with salt and just warm through.

4 Slice the rested steak on the diagonal, cutting away and discarding any fat if you prefer, then return to the pan with any juices, stirring to combine with the cream sauce. Heat the brandy in a ladle over a gentle flame and wait until it ignites, then pour over the steak mixture, stirring to mix. Spoon on to serving plates and serve at once with the chips and watercress salad.

13 Beef in Stout with Dumplings

No. 3 BEST OF BRITISH

SERVES 6–8

2 tbsp sunflower oil

50 g/2 oz unsalted butter

1.75 kg/4 lb chuck or blade beef steak, cut into 5-cm/2-in pieces

1 heaped tbsp plain flour

225 g/8 oz bacon lardons

450 g/1 lb shallots, peeled

1 tbsp Dijon mustard

2 tbsp dark muscovado sugar

175 g/6 oz ready-to-eat prunes, cut in half

175 g/6 oz pickled walnuts, cut into quarters

1 litre/1³/4 pints stout

900 ml /1¹/2 pints fresh beef stock (from a carton is fine)

salt and freshly ground black pepper

glazed carrots and steamed leeks, to serve

2 bouquet garni sachets

1 quantity *Dumplings* (p. 118), to serve

This is wonderful for cold days and perfect for serving large groups so that you can relax and enjoy the company with no last-minute hurdles. The flavours only improve if you make it a day ahead: just reheat it gently before popping on the dumplings to cook. Cuts like chuck or blade have that all-important gelatinous material which dissolves during the long cooking process and makes the meat magnificently succulent.

1 Preheat oven to 140°C/275°F/Gas 1; fan oven 120°C from cold. Heat the oil and butter in a large, non-stick frying pan. Place the beef in a large bowl and sprinkle over the flour and seasoning. Toss until lightly coated, shaking off any excess. Add half of the beef to the pan and cook until the meat is lightly browned.

2 Remove the beef from the pan with a slotted spoon and transfer to a casserole dish. Repeat with the remaining beef.

3 Add the bacon lardons to the pan and cook until sizzling and golden brown. Add the shallots and cook for another 2–3 minutes, stirring.

4 Meanwhile, add the mustard, sugar, prunes and pickled walnuts to the beef in the casserole dish, then tip in the bacon lardons and shallots, stirring to combine.

5 Pour about a quarter of the stout into the pan and allow to bubble down, scraping the bottom of the pan to remove any sediment. Pour into the casserole dish.

6 Stir the rest of the stout and the beef stock into the casserole dish. Pop the bouquet garni sachets into the casserole and season to taste. Bring to the boil, then cover and place in the oven. Cook for 5–6 hours until the beef is completely tender but still holding its shape.

7 Remove the cooked stew from the oven, season to taste and place the dumplings (see p. 118) on top. Increase the oven temperature to 180°C/350°F/Gas 4; fan oven160°. Return the casserole to the oven and cook, uncovered, for another 35–40 minutes until the dumplings have risen and are golden brown. Sprinkle over the remaining parsley and serve directly from the casserole with bowls of the glazed carrots and steamed leeks.

14 Steak and Kidney Pudding

SERVES 6–8

750 g/1¹/₂ lb chuck or blade beef steak, cut into 2.5-cm/1-in cubes

225 g/8 oz ox kidney, cut into 2.5-cm/1-in cubes

1 small onion, finely chopped

large pinch celery salt

1 tsp fresh thyme leaves

2 tbsp plain flour

150 ml/¹/₄ pint fresh beef stock (from a carton is fine)

salt and freshly ground black pepper

mashed potatoes and buttered peas, to serve

FOR THE SUET PASTRY:

400 g/14 oz self-raising flour, plus extra for dusting

200 g/7 oz beef or vegetarian suet

300 ml/¹/₂ pt water

unsalted butter, for greasing

This English classic, which you voted into 1st place, is one of the great all-time treats on a chilly evening. In the early nineteenth century a dozen or so oysters were used to add richness to the sauce. In the East End of London it is still referred to as a Kate and Sidney pudding, or a John Bull if it has been made with just steak and no kidney. Whatever you decide to call it, it really is the ultimate in comfort food!

1 Place the steak and kidney in a large bowl. Stir in the onion, celery salt, thyme leaves and seasoning. Toss together lightly and set to one side, or cover with cling film and chill for up to 24 hours to allow the flavours to combine.

2 To make the suet pastry, sift the flour and ¹/₂ teaspoon salt into a large bowl. Add the suet and season with pepper. Lightly mix and then add 300 ml/¹/₂ pint cold water a little at a time, cutting through the dough with a round-bladed knife as if you were making scones. Using your hands, mix to form a soft dough.

3 Roll out the pastry on a lightly floured work surface into a round approximately 5 mm–1 cm/¹/₄–¹/₂ in thick. Cut out one quarter of the pastry to within 2.5 cm/ 1 in of the centre; set aside for the lid. Use the remainder of the pastry to line a well-buttered 1.75-litre/3-pint pudding basin, leaving at least 1 cm/¹/₂ in of the pastry hanging over the edge.

4 Add the flour to the steak and kidney mixture and stir gently to combine. Place batches of the meat mixture into a sieve (with a glass bowl underneath) and shake to remove any excess flour. Spoon the lightly coated meat mixture into the lined pudding basin, being careful not to press it down, then pour in enough of the beef stock to come up nearly two-thirds to the top but not covering the meat completely.

5 Roll out the remaining pastry to a circle 2.5 cm/1 in larger than the top of the basin. Dampen the edges of the pastry lining the basin, place the lid over the filling and press the two edges together to seal; trim off any excess pastry. Make two small slits in the top.

6 Cover the pudding with a double piece of buttered foil, pleated in the centre to allow room for expansion while cooking. Now secure it with string, making a

handle so that you can easily lift it out of the hot steamer. Place the pudding on an upturned plate in a large pan filled two-thirds up the side of the basin with hot water. Steam for 5 hours, topping up with boiling water occasionally so as not to allow the pan to boil dry. When steamed, remove from the pan.

7 Remove from the pan, cut the string from the basin and remove the foil. Then wrap in a folded clean napkin to serve with mashed potatoes and buttered peas.

15 Beef Wellington

SERVES 6–8

a little olive oil

15 g/$^1/_2$ oz unsalted butter

1.5 kg/3 lb piece beef fillet

375 g/13 oz ready-rolled puff pastry, thawed if frozen

plain flour, for dusting

4 ready-made pancakes or crêpes

175 g/6 oz chicken liver pâté

1 small egg (preferably free-range or organic), beaten

salt and freshly ground black pepper

steamed purple sprouting broccoli or asparagus, to serve

FOR THE MUSHROOM STUFFING:

50 g/2 oz unsalted butter

150 g/5 oz shallots, finely diced

250 g/9 oz flat mushrooms, finely chopped

3 tbsp double cream

This is a wonderful combination of tender beef fillet, chicken liver pâté, concentrated mushrooms and a very crisp crust. The pastry helps to keep the meat really moist so that none of the aroma or juices can escape. The dish can be prepared several hours in advance and just popped into the oven once your guests arrive.

1 Heat the olive oil and the butter in a non-stick frying pan. Season the beef. When the pan is hot, add the beef and quickly seal all over. Remove from the pan, place on a plate and allow to cool completely.

2 To make the mushroom stuffing, heat the butter in the frying pan until hot and foaming, add the shallots and cook until softened and lightly golden. Add the mushrooms and cook gently, stirring until all the liquid evaporates. Add the cream to the pan and season generously. Continue to heat gently until the mixture has reduced to a thick purée. Set aside to cool completely.

3 Preheat the oven to 230°C/450°F/Gas 8; fan oven 210°C from cold. Roll out the pastry on a lightly floured work surface to fit the beef comfortably and lay two of the pancakes or crêpes on top, slightly overlapping. Spread a strip of chicken liver pâté across the centre of the pancakes – to the same width as the beef fillet.

4 Make a cut into the centre of the beef about three-quarters of the way through and fill with the cooled mushroom stuffing. Place the beef on the pancakes and cover with the remaining two pancakes, slightly overlapping. Cut away the middle of the ends of the pastry. Fold the long edges of the pastry over the meat and then neatly fold in the ends, dampening the edges to seal.

5 Place the wrapped beef fillet seam-side down on a large, non-stick baking sheet. Decorate the top with the pastry trimmings, if desired, and brush all over with the beaten egg. Place in the oven for 10 minutes, then reduce the heat to 190°C/375°F/Gas 5/ fan oven 170°C and continue to cook for another 20 minutes until the pastry is puffed up and golden brown. Remove from the oven to a carving board and allow to rest for 5 minutes before carving into thick slices. Serve at once with the steamed purple sprouting broccoli or asparagus.

16 Calf's Liver and Pancetta with Balsamic Vinegar

SERVES 4

4 small vines of cherry tomatoes, each with about 5 tomatoes

1–2 tbsp olive oil

50 g/2 oz piece pancetta, thinly sliced into six rashers

1 tbsp plain flour

4 x 175 g/6 oz calf's liver slices, each about 1 cm/$^1/_2$ in thick

50 g/2 oz unsalted butter

120 g/4$^1/_2$ oz pancetta cubes

2 shallots, finely chopped

2 tbsp balsamic vinegar

salt and freshly ground black pepper

1 heaped tbsp snipped fresh chives, to garnish

Artichoke Rösti, to serve (p. 112)

Calf's liver is undoubtedly the star of the offal world, wonderfully tender and delicately flavoured. Pancetta is basically Italian streaky bacon, but because of its flavourful curing it is quite superior – drier, purer and much tastier. However, if you can't get hold of it, replace the thinly sliced pancetta with streaky bacon rashers and the cubes with a piece of bacon chopped into lardons.

1 Preheat the oven to 180°C/350°F/Gas 4; fan oven 160°C from cold. Arrange the tomatoes in a small roasting tin and drizzle over the olive oil. Season generously and roast for 5–10 minutes until lightly charred.

2 Meanwhile, arrange the pancetta rashers on a wire rack set over a baking sheet and place in the oven until crisp and lightly golden – about 15-20 minutes.

3 Place the flour on a flat plate and season generously, then use to dust the calf's liver until well coated.

4 Heat a frying pan, then add 15 g/$^1/_2$ oz of the butter. Add the calf's liver to the pan and quickly fry for 2–3 minutes on each side, until golden brown. The liver should be pink in the centre, but if you prefer it well done cook for slightly longer.

5 Remove the liver from the pan, place on a plate and keep warm. Add the rest of the butter to the pan, then tip in the pancetta cubes and shallots. Cook over a medium heat until the shallots have softened, stirring occasionally.

6 Pour the balsamic vinegar into the pan, scraping the bottom to release any of the bits that have stuck. Cook for a minute and season to taste, then return the liver to the pan and just warm through.

7 Arrange the liver on serving plates with the roasted tomatoes and a couple of the crisp pancetta rashers. Add the *Artichoke Rösti*. Drizzle around a little of the balsamic sauce and garnish with the chives to serve.

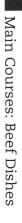

17 Roast Rib of Beef on the Bone

No. 1 CLASSIC DISHES

SERVES 6–8

1 tsp dried thyme

1 tsp dried basil

$1/2$ tsp cayenne pepper

1 tsp paprika

1 tsp garlic salt

$1/2$ tsp English mustard powder

2 kg/4$1/2$ lb piece fore-rib beef, on the bone

2 tbsp Dijon mustard

3 tbsp olive oil

1 onion, roughly chopped

1 carrot, roughly chopped

1 leek, roughly chopped

150 ml/$1/4$ pint red wine

600 ml/1 pint fresh beef stock (from a carton is fine)

salt and freshly ground black pepper

selection of vegetables, *Perfect roast potatoes* (p. 116), *Yorkshire Puddings* (p. 109) and *Horseradish Cream* (p. 118), to serve

You can't get much more British than roast beef and Yorkshire pudding! For me the best bit of Sunday lunch is the gear accompanying the beef: crusty potatoes, caramelized turnips and carrots, melting onions and pungent garlic – and, of course, *Yorkshire Puddings* and *Horseradish Cream* are vital.

1 Place the thyme, basil, cayenne, paprika, garlic salt and mustard powder into a bowl and mix to combine. Spread a thin layer of the Dijon mustard all over the fat side of the beef joint. Sprinkle the spice mixture on top, patting it down gently to help it stick.

2 Preheat the oven 200°C/400°F/Gas 6; fan oven 180°C. Pour the oil into a roasting tin and allow to heat in the oven for 5 minutes. Add the onion, carrot and leek, tossing to coat them in the oil. Season to taste and roast for 20 minutes until lightly caramelized.

3 Increase the oven temperature to 220°C/425°F/Gas 7; fan oven 200°C. Transfer the beef to the roasting tin using the vegetables as a bed to sit it on.

4 Add the red wine to the roasting tin with half of the stock. Roast for 15 minutes until well sealed, then reduce the oven temperature to 200°C/400°F/Gas 6/ fan oven 180°C again and continue to roast for 10 minutes per 450 g/1 lb for very rare, almost 'blue' meat, or 12 minutes per 450 g/1 lb for medium-rare, or 20–25 minutes per 450 g/1 lb for well-done. Remove meat from the roasting tin and place on a large dish. Allow the meat to rest in a warm place for at least 10–15 minutes before carving. If you carve straight from the oven, all the juices will end up in your dish.

5 Meanwhile, make the gravy. Pour the remaining stock into the roasting tin and place directly on the hob to heat. Cook for 5 minutes, stirring to combine and scraping the bottom with a wooden spoon to remove any sediment. Season to taste and pour the gravy through a sieve into a sauce boat.

7 Carve the beef into slices and arrange on serving plates with the vegetables, roast potatoes, *Yorkshire Puddings* and *Horseradish Cream*. Serve at once with the gravy to hand around separately.

18 Fillet Steak with Salsa Verde

SERVES 4

2 handfuls fresh flatleaf parsley leaves

12 fresh basil leaves

1 small handful fresh mint leaves

2 pickled baby gherkins

3 garlic cloves, peeled

2 tbsp capers, drained and rinsed

4 canned anchovy fillets, drained

1 tbsp red wine vinegar

1 tbsp lemon juice

1 tbsp Dijon mustard

7 tbsp extra-virgin olive oil

4 x 150 g/5 oz fillet steaks

Maldon sea salt and freshly ground black pepper

boiled new potatoes, to serve

Salsa verde is a great Italian sauce that is excellent served with a good fillet steak and some chunky red wine. It also goes wonderfully with grilled fish, or tongue which is traditional in Italy. It needs to taste very fresh, so don't make it too far in advance. I think that you get a better product if you hand-chop when preparing salsa, but you can always pulse it in the food processor if you're short of time.

1 Coarsely chop the parsley, basil, mint and cucumbers by hand with the garlic, capers and anchovy fillets, or pulse in a food processor.

2 Transfer to a non-metallic bowl and gradually whisk in the vinegar, lemon juice, mustard and 6 tablespoons of the oil. Season with $1/2$ teaspoon salt and $1/4$ teaspoon pepper. This quantity should make about 250 ml/8 fl oz in total. Set aside, covered with cling film, at room temperature.

3 Heat a heavy-based frying pan. Add the remaining oil and then add the steaks and cook for 2–4 minutes on each side, depending on how rare you like your steak. Transfer the steaks to a plate, season to taste and set aside in a warm place to rest for about 5 minutes. Arrange the steaks on serving plates and spoon some of the salsa verde to the side. Serve at once with the boiled new potatoes.

19 Steak Cacciatore

SERVES 4

1 tbsp olive oil

450 g/1 lb piece sirloin or rump steak, about 4 cm/1¹/₂ in thick

350 g/12 oz dried rigatoni pasta

2 shallots, finely chopped

2 garlic cloves, crushed

¹/₂ tsp chopped fresh thyme

1 fresh bay leaf

100 g/4 oz streaky bacon lardons

400 g/14 oz can pimientos in brine, drained, rinsed and cut into long, thin strips

50 g/2 oz pitted black olives

350 g/12 oz jar puttanesca sauce

100 g/4 oz mixed mushrooms, sliced

1 tbsp chopped fresh oregano

salt and freshly ground black pepper

This easy sauce for pasta can also be served with chicken or fish, instead of steak. The sauce can be made well in advance, then reheated gently and folded into the sliced steak before serving on a bed of rigatoni pasta. There's a debate about which is better – dried or fresh pasta, and I can honestly say that I think dried pasta is better for most recipes. It uses a hard durum wheat, which when cooked properly gives that lovely 'bite' that we talk about when cooking pasta. My wife suggests that you throw a piece of pasta at a wall to test if it is cooked – if it sticks, it is ready to eat, but then she is Irish!

1 Heat the oil in a heavy-based frying pan over a high heat. Add the steak and cook for 2 minutes on each side, then reduce the heat and continue to cook for 5–10 minutes, turning once, depending on how rare you like your steak. Transfer the steak to a plate, season to taste with salt and set aside in a warm place to rest.

2 At the same time, bring a large pan of water to a rolling boil. Add a good pinch of salt and tip in the rigatoni, stir once and cook for 8–12 minutes or according to the packet instructions until the pasta is al dente.

3 Add the shallots to the pan in which you cooked the steak, with the garlic, thyme and bay leaf. Cook for 2 minutes, stirring, then add the bacon lardons and continue to cook until sizzling but not browned. Add the pimientos and olives and cook for a further 2 minutes. Stir in the puttanesca sauce and then add the mushrooms and oregano. Season and continue to cook until the mushrooms are tender, stirring occasionally.

4. Slice the rested steak on the diagonal, cutting away and discarding any fat, if you prefer, then return to the pan with any juices, stirring to combine with the sauce. Drain the pasta, quickly refresh under cold running water and divide among serving bowls. Spoon over the steak and sauce and serve at once.

20 Spaghetti Bolognese

No. 7 CLASSIC DISHES

SERVES 6

about 150 ml/¼ pint olive oil

50 g/2 oz streaky bacon, diced

1 onion, finely diced

1 celery stick, finely diced

1 carrot, finely diced

2 garlic cloves, crushed

1 tsp fresh soft thyme leaves

1 bay leaf

1 tsp dried oregano

400 g/14 oz can chopped tomatoes

1 tbsp tomato purée

1½ tsp anchovy essence

1 tbsp Worcestershire sauce

900 g/2 lb minced beef (coarsely ground, if possible)

100 g/4 oz fresh chicken livers, finely chopped

1 bottle dry red wine

1 litre/1¾ pints fresh chicken, beef or lamb stock (from a carton is fine)

450g/1 lb dried spaghetti

salt and freshly ground black pepper

freshly grated Parmesan cheese, to garnish

My Bolognese sauce is slightly different: I like adding some diced chicken livers for extra richness and – my secret ingredients – anchovy essence and Worcestershire sauce. It is a great freezer standby. I normally make double and then freeze it in smaller batches.

1 Heat a large, heavy-based pan. Add 2 tablespoons of the oil and tip in the bacon. Cook for a couple of minutes until it is crispy and has released some natural fats, then add the onion, celery, carrot, garlic, thyme, bay leaf and oregano and cook over a medium heat until the vegetables have softened and taken on a little colour, stirring occasionally. Add the canned tomatoes, tomato purée, anchovy essence and Worcestershire sauce. Stir to combine and season to taste.

2 Meanwhile, heat a large frying pan. Add a little of the oil and fry the minced beef in small batches until browned. While the meat is frying, break up any lumps with the back of a wooden spoon. Repeat until all the beef is browned. Drain off any fat and stir the meat into the tomato mixture.

3 Wipe out the pan with some kitchen paper and add a little more oil, then fry the chicken livers until sizzling and lightly browned. Tip into the minced beef mixture, then deglaze the frying pan with some of the red wine, scraping any sediment from the bottom with a wooden spoon. Pour this wine, along with the rest of the wine and the stock, into the minced beef mixture, stirring to combine.

4 Bring to the boil, then reduce the heat and simmer, stirring from time to time for about 2 hours (up to 4 hours is fine) until the beef is completely tender. Season to taste. If the liquid reduces too much, top up with a little water. If time allows, leave to cool, then chill until the fat solidifies on the top. Carefully remove it and discard.

5 To serve, reheat the Bolognese sauce in a pan over a gentle heat. Bring a large pan of water to a rolling boil. Add a good pinch of salt and a dash of the olive oil. Swirl in the spaghetti, stir once and cook for 8-12 minutes or according to the packet instructions until the pasta is al dente. Drain and quickly refresh under cold running water, then divide among serving bowls. Spoon over the sauce, sprinkle over some Parmesan and serve at once.

21 Ballymaloe Irish Stew

1.25 kg/2½ lb lamb chops (gigot or rack), not less than 2.5 cm/1 in thick

6 onions, cut into quarters (through the root)

6 carrots, cut into large chunks

750–900 ml/1¼–1½ pints fresh lamb or chicken stock (or water)

8–12 potatoes (more if you like!)

1 fresh thyme sprig

1 tbsp softened butter (optional), plus extra for greasing

1 tbsp plain flour (optional)

1 tbsp chopped fresh flatleaf parsley

1 tbsp snipped fresh chives

salt and freshly ground black pepper

Having married an Irish girl, I've been subjected to Irish stew in its most basic form, and though obviously you can add other ingredients, such as leeks, turnips and pearl barley, they are not traditional, as my good friend Darina Allen would be only too happy to tell you. This is her version of the Irish classic and I have to agree it's probably the best I've ever tasted. Try it on a cold winter's day and you'll not be disappointed.

1 Preheat the oven to 180°C/350°F/Gas 4; fan oven 160°C from cold. Cut the chops in half and trim off all the excess fat, then render down the fat over a gentle heat in a heavy-based frying pan. Discard the rendered-down pieces. Toss the chops into the pan and cook until lightly browned, turning occasionally. Transfer to a plate, then quickly toss the onions in the fat followed by the carrots.

2 Build up the lamb, onions and carrots in layers in a large, flameproof casserole dish, seasoning each layer as you go. Deglaze the pan with the stock, scraping the bottom with a wooden spoon to remove any sediment, and pour into the casserole.

3 Lay the potatoes on top, so they can steam while the stew cooks. Season, then add the thyme and bring to the boil on top of the stove. Cover with a butter wrapper or buttered paper lid and then cover with the lid of the casserole. Transfer to the oven or allow to simmer on top of the stove for 1–1½ hours until the stew is cooked through and completely tender.

4 When the stew is cooked, carefully pour off the cooking liquid into another pan, skim off the grease and reheat gently. If you want to thicken the sauce slightly, you can make a roux with the butter and flour. Simply melt the butter in a small pan and stir in the flour, then cook for 1–2 minutes on a low heat, stirring. Whisk into the sauce, a little at a time, until you have achieved the desired consistency. Season to taste and add the parsley and chives. Pour the sauce back into the casserole and bring back to boiling point on top of the stove. Serve straight from the pot or in a large terracotta dish.

22 Butterflied Lamb with Moroccan Mint Mechoui

SERVES 4–6

3 kg/7 lb leg of lamb, boned and well trimmed, roughly 4–5 cm/1^{1}/$_{2}$–2 in thick

25 g/1 oz chopped fresh mint, plus extra to garnish

juice of 2 lemons

4 garlic cloves, finely chopped

2 tbsp ground coriander

2 tsp paprika

2 tsp ground cumin

2 tsp coarsely ground black pepper

1 tsp cayenne pepper

4 tbsp extra-virgin olive oil

salt

Jewelled Couscous (p. 113) and green salad, to serve

This butterflied leg of lamb is excellent for grilling on the barbie. It may seem like I've used a lot of mint and spices, but trust me: the final flavour is actually quite subtle. Do try to marinate the meat overnight for added flavour. When you are buying the lamb, ask the butcher to remove the parchment-like covering on the skin, and to cut out the bone – this will ensure more even cooking and make it much easier to carve.

1 Place the lamb in a shallow, non-metallic dish. Mix together all of the remaining ingredients except the salt and rub all over the meat. Cover tightly with cling film and chill overnight or leave to stand at room temperature for 2–3 hours if time is short.

2 Preheat the oven to 240°C/475°F/Gas 9; fan oven 210°C from cold. If the lamb has been chilled overnight, bring it back to room temperature. Place the lamb, cut-side up, on a rack in a large roasting tin and season with salt. Roast for 15 minutes, then turn over and roast for another 10 minutes for rare. Alternatively, cook on a BBQ with a domed lid, such as a Weber.

3 Remove the lamb from the oven and leave to rest in a warm place for 10 minutes. If you don't like your lamb too pink, you can cover it with foil at this point and it will continue to cook. Carve into slices, garnish with chopped mint and serve at once with *Jewelled Couscous* and salad.

23 Moroccan Lamb Tagine

No. 5   HOLIDAY DISHES

SERVES 6–8

1¹/₂ tbsp ground ginger

2 tsp ground black pepper

2 tbsp ground cinnamon

1 tbsp ground turmeric

1¹/₂ tbsp paprika

1 tsp cayenne pepper

1 lamb shoulder, knuckle removed, cut into 5-cm/2-in pieces: you'll need 1.25 kg/ 2¹/₂ lb in total

2 tbsp olive oil and 2 tbsp argan oil

2 large onions, grated

3 garlic cloves, crushed

100 g/4 oz ready-to-eat dried apricots, cut in half

50 g/2 oz dates, cut in half

75 g/3 oz flaked almonds

50 g/2 oz sultanas or raisins

1 tbsp clear honey

1 tsp saffron, pre-soaked

600 ml/1 pint tomato juice

600 ml/1 pint fresh lamb or chicken stock (from a carton is fine)

400 g/14 oz can tomatoes

2 tbsp chopped fresh coriander

2 tbsp chopped fresh flatleaf parsley

Jewelled Couscous (p. 113), to serve

I like to make my tagines a little richer than is traditional in Morocco. This involves browning the meat, frying off the spices, reducing the sauce and cooking it all gently in the oven. The flavour of this tagine only improves with time: just leave it to cool completely, then place in the fridge for up to 2 days. This also allows any excess fat to rise to the top so that it can be easily removed. Don't go boning out a shoulder of lamb – get your butcher to do it for you; that's their job. Argan oil is a Moroccan oil from the argan tree, which you should be able to find in specialist shops, or you could just use olive oil.

1 Preheat the oven to 150˚C/300˚F/Gas 2; fan oven 130˚C from cold. Place the ginger, black pepper, cinnamon, turmeric, paprika and cayenne in a small bowl and mix to combine, then tip half into a large bowl. Add the lamb pieces and toss until evenly coated. Cover with cling film and chill overnight if time allows.

2 Heat a large, flameproof casserole dish and add 1 tablespoon of the olive oil and 1 tablespoon of the argan oil. Tip in half of the lamb and cook over a medium heat until evenly browned but not scorched, then tip on to a plate. Repeat until all of the lamb has been browned. Add the remaining olive and argan oil to the casserole and stir in the remaining spice mixture and the onions and cook for 6–8 minutes, stirring occasionally. Add the garlic and continue to cook for 2–3 minutes, stirring, until the onions are softened but not browned.

3 Add the browned lamb pieces to the casserole with the apricots, dates, almonds, sultanas or raisins, honey, saffron mixture, tomato juice and stock. Bring to the boil, then transfer to the oven and cook for 1 hour. Stir in the chopped tomatoes, and cook for another hour or until the lamb is completely tender but still holding its shape and the sauce has thickened. To serve, transfer the lamb to a tagine or large serving dish and sprinkle over the coriander and parsley. Serve hot with the *Jewelled Couscous*.

24 Moussaka

No. 4 HOLIDAY DISHES

SERVES 6–8

175 ml/6 fl oz olive oil

1 large onion, finely chopped

3 garlic cloves, finely chopped

750 g/1¹/₂ lb minced lamb

175 ml/6 fl oz white wine

¹/₄ tsp ground cinnamon

¹/₄ tsp ground allspice

1 tbsp chopped fresh oregano

2 fresh bay leaves

1 tsp fresh soft thyme leaves

2 x 400 g/14 oz cans chopped tomatoes

4 aubergines

plain flour, for dusting

a chunky tomato, cucumber, parsley and mint salad with crusty bread, to serve

FOR THE BÉCHAMEL SAUCE:

75 g/3 oz unsalted butter

75 g/3 oz plain flour

900 ml/1¹/₂ pints milk

75 g/3 oz Parmesan cheese, freshly grated

100 g/4 oz Gruyère cheese, grated

1 egg, plus 2 egg yolks (preferably free-range or organic)

salt and freshly ground pepper

Moussaka is one of those dishes that has been unfairly derided. Some restaurants in Greece have been known to make dishes like moussaka in the morning, and then the dishes sit in hot cabinets all day until unsuspecting tourists eat them in the evening. The Greeks themselves quite sensibly eat moussaka freshly made at lunchtime. Eat it fresh and it is as good as, if not better than, our own favourite shepherd's pie. However, this dish can be prepared in advance until the point before it goes in the oven. Allow an extra 15 minutes in the oven if cooking from cold.

1 Heat 2 tablespoons of the oil in a large saucepan. Add the onion and cook gently for 6–8 minutes, stirring occasionally. Add the garlic and cook for another 2–3 minutes until the onion is softened but not coloured, stirring occasionally.

2 Meanwhile, heat a frying pan. Add a little of the oil, tip in half the minced lamb and cook over a fairly high heat until evenly browned, breaking up any lumps with a wooden spoon, then tip on to a plate. Repeat until all of the lamb has been cooked, then deglaze the pan with a little of the white wine, scraping the bottom with a wooden spoon to remove any sediment.

3 Stir the cinnamon into the onion mixture in the saucepan with the allspice, oregano, bay leaves and thyme and cook for a minute or so, stirring. Add the cooked lamb and the reduced wine, along with the remaining wine and the chopped tomatoes. Bring to the boil, then reduce the heat and simmer for 1 hour or until the lamb is completely tender and the sauce is slightly reduced.

4 Meanwhile, cut the aubergines into 1-cm/¹/₂-in slices, then layer up in a colander, sprinkling with salt as you go. Set aside on the draining board of the sink for 30 minutes to allow the salt to draw out any bitter juices.

5 To make the béchamel sauce, melt the butter in a non-stick pan and stir in the flour. Remove from the heat and gradually stir in the milk, then return the pan to the heat. Cook for 6–8 minutes, stirring continuously, until the sauce is smooth and thickened. Remove from the heat and stir in 50 g/2 oz of the Parmesan and

contd. overleaf

50 g/2 oz of the Gruyère until melted. Season to taste and set aside to cool a little, then whisk in the egg and egg yolks to combine.

6 Heat a large frying pan. Rinse the aubergine slices under cold running water and pat dry with plenty of kitchen paper. Dust the aubergine slices with the flour. Add a couple of tablespoons of the oil to the frying pan and fry the aubergine slices in batches, adding more oil as necessary, for 8–10 minutes until cooked through and golden, turning once. Drain on kitchen paper. You are now ready to construct the moussaka.

7 Preheat the oven to 180°C/350°F/Gas 4; fan oven 160°C from cold. Spoon a third of the lamb mixture into the base of an ovenproof dish that is about 30 x 20 cm/12 x 8 in, discarding the bay leaves. Cover with half of the aubergine slices. Repeat the layers, finishing with a layer of the lamb mixture, then pour over the cheese sauce. Sprinkle the remaining Parmesan and Gruyère on top and bake for 50 minutes –1 hour, until bubbling and golden brown. Allow the moussaka to settle for 5 minutes before cutting into squares and serving with the salad and crusty bread.

25 Tuscan-style Lamb

SERVES 2

6 x 75 g/3 oz lamb noisettes

4 garlic cloves, 2 cut into 9 slivers and 2 finely chopped

9 tiny fresh rosemary sprigs

4 tbsp extra-virgin olive oil

1 onion, finely chopped

2 carrots, diced

2 celery sticks, diced

1 heaped tsp fresh thyme leaves

4 canned anchovy fillets, drained and finely chopped

1 glass red wine, about 120 ml/4 fl oz

300 ml/1/2 pint fresh lamb or chicken stock (from a carton is fine)

400 g/14 oz can chopped tomatoes

1 tbsp tomato purée

400 g/14 oz can cannellini beans, drained and rinsed

2 tbsp chopped fresh flatleaf parsley

salt and freshly ground black pepper

English lamb is available from early spring (from winter-born lambs of southern England) through to the end of summer (from lambs born in the highlands of Scotland and the mountains of Wales) and is just perfect for this dish. Noisettes are boned and rolled lamb steaks made from the rack of lamb – try to buy them with rosy pink flesh and a good coating of creamy white fat that is firm to the touch. You should seal the noisettes over a high heat, then reduce the temperature to finish cooking.

1 Make three small incisions in the skin of each noisette. Insert the garlic slivers and rosemary sprigs. Season with pepper. Place in a non-metallic dish and drizzle over half of the oil. Cover with cling film and leave for 15 minutes at room temperature or up to 24 hours in the fridge.

2 Heat a sauté pan. Add the remaining oil and fry the onion, carrots, celery and thyme over a high heat for about 10 minutes, stirring regularly, until softened and lightly browned, then stir in the finely chopped garlic and anchovies.

3 Pour in the wine, scraping the bottom of the pan with a wooden spoon to release any sediment, then add the stock, chopped tomatoes and tomato purée. Season, bring to the boil, then reduce the heat and simmer for 15–20 minutes until well reduced and thickened, stirring occasionally.

4 Heat a griddle pan, barbecue or grill. Shake any excess oil from the noisettes and add to the pan of your choice. Cook for 3–4 minutes on each side until lightly charred and just rare. Season with salt and carefully snip away the string from each noisette.

5 Add the beans and most of the parsley to the tomato mixture and stir to combine. Season and cook for 5 minutes until heated through. Spoon into wide-rimmed bowls, garnish with the rest of the parsley and arrange the lamb noisettes on top to serve.

26 Rack of Lamb with a Pistachio Crust

SERVES 4–6

2 x 7-bone best ends of lamb, each about 275–350 g/ 10–12 oz

about 1 tbsp prepared English mustard

Potato and Turnip Bake **(p.111) and steamed asparagus, to serve**

FOR THE PISTACHIO CRUST:

25 g/1 oz unsalted butter

50 g/2 oz shelled pistachio nuts

2 tbsp fresh soft thyme leaves

2 tbsp snipped fresh chives

2 tbsp chopped fresh flatleaf parsley

50 g/2 oz fresh white bread-crumbs

finely grated rind of $1/2$ lemon

1 small garlic clove, roughly chopped

salt and freshly ground black pepper

Adapt this traditional dish with aromatic herbs and a fantastic pistachio crust. Spring is the time of year when British products start to come into their own: wonderful new-season lamb served with English asparagus and the first crop of potatoes. Foods seem to taste so much better when eaten in their true seasons. Ask your butcher to French-trim the racks of lamb for you, and if he doesn't know what that is, tell him to remove the meat and fat from the rib bones, leaving 5–6 cm/2–2$1/2$ in of clean bones exposed.

1 Preheat the oven to 200°C/400°F/Gas 6; fan oven 180°C from cold. To make the pistachio crust, melt the butter in a small pan or in the microwave. Place in a food processor with the pistachio nuts and herbs and blitz until bright green. Add the breadcrumbs, lemon rind, garlic and seasoning and blend again for just a few seconds until all the ingredients are well combined.

2 Place the racks of lamb on a chopping board and, using a pastry brush, spread the mustard thickly over the fat side of each rack. Cover with the pistachio crust using your hands to mould it over the lamb. Arrange the lamb, coated-side up, on a baking sheet and chill for at least 30 minutes (up to 2 hours is fine) to allow the crust to 'set'.

3 Place the racks of lamb in a small roasting tin and roast for 20–25 minutes, or a little longer, depending on how pink you like your lamb. Remove the lamb from the oven and set aside in a warm place to rest for 10–15 minutes, then carve into chops and serve with the *Potato and Turnip Bake* and steamed asparagus.

27 Lancashire Hotpot

SERVES 4

4 lambs' kidneys, skinned

8 x 175 g/6 oz lamb chump chops, excess fat removed

1 heaped tbsp plain flour

1 tbsp beef dripping or sunflower oil

600 ml/1 pint fresh lamb stock (from a carton is fine)

75 g/3 oz unsalted butter

1.25 kg/2$^{1}/_{2}$ lb floury potatoes, such as King Edward

4 fresh thyme sprigs

2 onions, thinly sliced

2 fresh bay leaves

salt and freshly ground black pepper

steamed broccoli and glazed carrots, to serve

It's scrummy, it's fantastic and it should be eaten more. I love food that you can just throw into a pot, turn on the heat and forget about. Use dripping instead of oil for a lovely depth of flavour. This dish is very cheap to produce for large numbers of people and simple to cook; you can leave it for 2$^{1}/_{2}$–3 hours and do something else, like have a drink! Sometimes I like to serve this just with chunks of crusty bread and a mug of tea or ale, but some fresh vegetables can make a welcome addition.

1 Preheat the oven to 180°C/350°F/Gas 4; fan oven 160°C from cold. Place the kidneys on a chopping board and cut each one in half, then use a small pair of scissors to remove the central core and membrane. Place in a bowl with the lamb chops, add the flour and season generously. Toss to coat, shaking off any excess.

2 Heat a large, non-stick frying pan. Add the dripping or oil and brown the chops for 2–3 minutes on each side – you may have to do this in batches depending on the size of the pan. Transfer to a plate and set aside. Add the kidneys to the pan and fry for 1–2 minutes on each side, then add to the plate with the chops. Tip away any excess fat from the pan and add a little of the stock to deglaze, scraping the bottom with a wooden spoon to remove any sediment.

3 Grease the inside of a 4.5-litre/8-pint heavy-based casserole dish with 25 g/1 oz of the butter. Cut 900 g/2 lb of the potatoes into 5-mm/$^{1}/_{4}$-in slices and thinly slice the remainder to use for the top of the hotpot. Line the bottom of the dish with half of the 5-mm/$^{1}/_{4}$-in potato slices. Place 4 of the chops on top, then add 2 of the thyme sprigs and half of the onions. Season to taste and pop the kidneys around the sides of the casserole dish. Repeat the layers with the remaining ingredients, tucking in the bay leaves, and pour over the stock used to deglaze the pan along with the rest of the stock.

4 Finally arrange an overlapping layer of the thinly sliced potatoes on top. Melt the remaining butter in a small pan or in the microwave and brush all over the potatoes. Add a sprinkling of salt, cover and bake in the oven for 2$^{1}/_{2}$ hours until the lamb is completely tender, removing the lid for the final 30 minutes to allow the potatoes to go golden brown. Serve the Lancashire hotpot straight from the casserole dish with bowls of the broccoli and carrots.

28 Shepherd's Pie

No.3 CLASSIC DISHES

SERVES 6-8

25 g/1 oz beef dripping or 2 tbsp sunflower oil

1 large onion, finely chopped

olive oil, for cooking

450 g/1 lb minced lamb

1 tbsp plain flour

2 fresh bay leaves

1 tsp chopped fresh thyme

1 tsp anchovy essence

200 g/7 oz can chopped tomatoes

250 ml/8 fl oz fresh lamb, chicken or beef stock (from a carton is fine)

2 tsp Worcestershire sauce

salt and freshly ground black pepper

buttered peas, to serve

FOR THE MASHED POTATOES:

750 g/1¹/₂ lb floury potatoes, such as Maris Piper, cut into chunks

50 ml/2 fl oz milk

75 g/3 oz unsalted butter

1 egg yolk (preferably free-range or organic)

This classic Shepherd's pie, voted third in the nation's top ten favourites, shows that people like food just like Mum used to cook. It should be made with lamb (hence the reference to shepherds), its sister dish, cottage pie, was made with the leftovers of the Sunday joint. I often serve a variation on the classic using pureéd cauliflower cheese instead of mashed potato. However, there's really no comparison to the real thing – just serve a big dollop and enjoy!

1 Heat a frying pan, add the dripping or oil, tip in the onion and cook for 5 minutes until softened but not browned, stirring occasionally.

2 Meanwhile, heat a large, heavy-based pan. Add a little olive oil, then tip in half of the minced lamb and cook over a fairly high heat until evenly browned, breaking up any lumps with a wooden spoon. Transfer to a plate. Repeat until all of the lamb has been cooked, then return all of the lamb to the pan and add the cooked onions, stirring to combine.

3 Sprinkle over the flour and add the bay leaves, thyme and anchovy essence, stirring to combine. Add the chopped tomatoes, stock, Worcestershire sauce and a good pinch of pepper. Bring to the boil, then reduce the heat, cover and simmer for 45 minutes–1 hour until the lamb is completely tender and softened. Season to taste. Allow to cool.

4 Preheat the oven to 180°C/350°F/Gas 4; fan oven 160°C from cold. Meanwhile, make the mashed potatoes. Place the potatoes in a pan of boiling salted water, cover and simmer for 15–20 minutes until tender. Drain and return to the pan for a couple of minutes to dry out, shaking the pan occasionally to prevent the potatoes sticking to the bottom. Mash the potatoes or pass through a potato ricer or vegetable mouli if you like a really smooth finish. Place in a large bowl and fold in the milk, butter and egg yolk. Season to taste.

5 Spoon the lamb mixture into a 1.75-litre/3-pint pie dish, discarding the bay leaves. Cover with the mashed potatoes, then smooth over and mark with a spatula or fork. Bake for 25–30 minutes until bubbling and golden brown. Serve at once, straight from the dish, with a bowl of peas.

29 Fingerlicking Ribs

SERVES 4–6

300 ml/¹/₂ pint tomato ketchup

300 ml/¹/₂ pint dark soy sauce

120 g/4¹/₂ oz clear honey

5-cm/2-in piece fresh root ginger, peeled and finely chopped

4 garlic cloves, finely chopped

5 tbsp amontillado sherry

1 tsp ground star anise (optional)

1 tbsp katchup manis (sweet soy sauce)

1 tbsp chopped fresh rosemary

1.75–2.25 kg/4–5 lb pork spare ribs (still joined and baby back, if possible)

2 spring onions, finely chopped

buttered mini corn cobs and *Crispy Potato Skins* (p. 117), to serve

Glorious, glorious ribs – lip-smackingly good. I like to use baby back ribs which you should be able to get from a good pork butcher, especially if you order them in advance. As they are from a young animal they are much smaller than normal ones, but still have plenty of meat with a much more succulent flavour. If you can't get hold of them, use ordinary ribs: just ask the butcher not to cut them into individual ribs. Katchup manis (also known as kecap manis), the sweet soy sauce used in this recipe, is available from oriental stores and larger supermarkets.

1 Place the tomato ketchup in a large, shallow dish with the soy sauce, honey, ginger, garlic, sherry, star anise (if using), katchup manis and rosemary, then mix thoroughly to combine. Add the ribs, cover with cling film and chill for up to 24 hours if time allows.

2 Place the ribs in a large, deep pan – you may have to cut them in half to get them to fit. Pour over the tomato ketchup mixture and add enough water to cover the ribs completely. Bring to a simmer, then cook over a medium heat for 45 minutes–1 hour until completely tender. Remove the ribs from the heat and transfer to a large, shallow, non-metallic dish. Allow them to cool in the marinade, then cover with cling film and chill until ready to grill.

3 Preheat the grill. When you want to use the ribs, carefully scoop off the fat from the top of the mixture and discard, then allow the mixture to come back up to room temperature. Drain off all the marinade, place in a pan and reduce down to a sticky coating consistency.

4 Arrange the ribs on a grill rack and cook for about 8 minutes on each side, basting or painting them occasionally with the reduced marinade. To serve, cut the ribs into single sections and arrange on a large platter, then scatter over the spring onions. Have the corn cobs and potato skins on the side or in separate bowls with plenty of napkins and finger bowls to hand for those sticky fingers.

30 Asian Pork in Lettuce Leaves

SERVES 4

4 garlic cloves, finely chopped

1 tsp salt

1 heaped tsp ground black
pepper

2 tbsp fresh lime juice

4 tbsp chopped fresh coriander

groundnut or sunflower oil, for
cooking

450 g/1 lb lean minced pork

4 tbsp chopped peanuts

4 tbsp chopped bamboo shoots

4 tbsp Thai fish sauce (nam
pla) or light soy sauce

2 tbsp clear honey

2 bird's eye chillies, finely
chopped

3 shallots, thinly sliced

2 large oranges, segmented

2 tbsp chopped fresh mint

4 Little Gem lettuces,
separated into leaves

Just as brown is the new black, believe it or not, pork is fast becoming the new chicken. Forget what you've been told about pork being fatty and unhealthy: it can be very lean, as in this dish. The same can't be said for the accompanying deep-fried shallots, but you could always leave them out and serve the filled lettuce leaves with the salad which contains lots of fresh, clean flavours.

1 Heat a large frying pan or wok. Mix together the garlic, salt, pepper, lime juice and half of the coriander in a small bowl. Add 2 tablespoons of the oil to the pan, tip in the garlic mixture and stir-fry for 30 seconds, then add the pork and stir-fry for 8–10 minutes until well browned, breaking up the mince as it cooks with a wooden spoon.

2 Add the peanuts, bamboo shoots, fish sauce or soy sauce, honey and chillies to the pork mixture and cook for another 5 minutes or until the liquid has almost completely evaporated, stirring occasionally.

3 Meanwhile, heat at least 5 cm/2 in of the oil to 375°F/190°C in a deep-sided pan or deep-fat fryer. Add two of the shallots to the heated oil and deep-fry for 30 seconds or so until crispy. Remove with a slotted spoon and drain well on kitchen paper.

4 Place the remaining shallot in a bowl with the orange segments and a heaped teaspoon each of the mint and coriander. Mix until well combined and pile into the middle of a large plate. Stir the remaining mint and coriander into the pork mixture and use to fill the lettuce leaves, arranging them around the orange salad. Scatter over the crispy shallots and serve at once.

31 Bacon and Pease Pudding

No. 5 BEST OF BRITISH

SERVES 8–10

6 carrots, peeled

6 onions, peeled with root intact

2.25 kg/5 lb unsmoked bacon collar, soaked overnight

2 celery hearts, trimmed and quartered lengthways

12 black peppercorns

2 fresh bay leaves

pared rind of 1 orange, studded with 4 whole cloves

6 fresh parsley stalks

12 new salad potatoes, such as Charlotte

12 baby leeks, trimmed

FOR THE PEASE PUDDING:

350 g/12 oz split yellow peas, well rinsed and soaked overnight

1 potato, roughly chopped

1 onion, cut into 4 wedges

2–3 fresh mint sprigs

75 g/3 oz unsalted butter, plus extra for greasing

1 egg (preferably free-range or organic)

4 tbsp chopped fresh flatleaf parsley

salt and freshly ground black pepper

Pease pudding is rarely made nowadays, but teamed up with the right vegetables, it's utterly delicious. The bacon needs to be soaked overnight, preferably in several changes of water – there's nothing worse than salty bacon. The stock that is created from boiling the bacon makes the most wonderful basis for a soup, so whatever you do, don't throw it out.

1 Put the carrots and onions into a large pan. Drain the bacon joint and place it on top of the vegetables. Add the celery, peppercorns, bay leaves and studded orange rind, then fill the pan with cold water to cover the bacon completely.

2 To make the pease pudding, drain and rinse the split peas, then tip into a large bowl lined with a large piece of muslin. Add the potato, onion and mint, mixing to combine. Tie to secure and pop into the pan with the bacon.

3 Add the parsley stalks to the pan and bring to the boil. Reduce the heat and simmer for 1 hour, removing any scum that rises to the top and topping up with boiling water as required to keep the bacon completely covered.

4 After an hour, remove the pease pudding from the pan and continue to cook the bacon. Open the muslin bag and tip the contents into a food processor, discarding the mint sprigs. Add the butter, egg and chopped parsley and season to taste. Blend to a smooth consistency.

5 Spoon the pease pudding into a well-buttered 1.2-litre/2-pint pudding basin and place a circle of buttered greaseproof paper on top. Cover the pudding with a double piece of foil, pleated in the centre to allow room for expansion while cooking. Now secure it with string, making a handle so that you can easily lift it out of a hot steamer. Place the pudding on an upturned plate in a large pan filled two-thirds up the side of the basin with hot water. Steam for 40–50 minutes, topping up with boiling water occasionally so that the pan does not boil dry.

6 After 45 minutes, by which time the bacon will have been cooking for 1 hour 45 minutes, add the new potatoes and leeks to the bacon. Continue to cook for

contd. overleaf

another 15 minutes or until the bacon, potatoes and leeks are all completely tender but still holding their shape.

7 Remove the bacon from the pan and place on a carving board. Snip away the string and cut away any excess fat, then carve the meat into thick slices. Invert the pease pudding basin on to a flat plate and cut the pudding into wedges. Arrange the bacon slices on serving plates with the pease pudding and spoon around a selection of the vegetables to serve.

32 Quiche Lorraine

SERVES 4

175 g/6 oz smoked streaky bacon lardons

2 eggs, plus 2 egg yolks (preferably free-range or organic)

250 ml/8 fl oz double cream

2 tbsp snipped fresh chives (optional)

pinch freshly grated nutmeg

salt and freshly ground black pepper

green salad, to serve

FOR THE PASTRY:

100 g/4 oz plain flour, plus extra for dusting

pinch salt

50 g/2 oz unsalted butter, chilled and cut into cubes, plus extra for greasing

1–2 tbsp iced water

1 egg yolk (preferably free-range or organic)

a little beaten egg, for glazing

A real quiche Lorraine is a delicate, subtle thing. I like to make pastry in the food processor as it's difficult to go wrong. Once it's rested, roll it out about 5 cm/2 in larger than the tin, then use the rolling pin to help you, lift the pastry over the tin. Lift the edges of the pastry so that they fall down into the tin, then gently press against the edges of the tin. Trim the edges with a sharp knife: it's that simple.

1 To make the pastry, place the butter, water and egg yolk in a food processor and blend until it resembles scrambled egg. Then tip in the flour and salt in one go and pulse in a food processor until the dough just comes together, without being overworked. Then knead gently on a lightly floured surface for a few seconds until smooth and firm. Place in a polythene bag and chill for at least 1 hour before rolling.

2 Roll out the pastry as thinly as possible on a lightly floured surface and use it to line a greased loose-bottomed 20-cm/8-in fluted flan tin that is about 4 cm/ 1³/₄ –2 in deep. Chill the pastry case for 30 minutes to let it rest and to reduce shrinkage during cooking.

3 Preheat the oven to 180°C/350°F/Gas 4; fan oven 160°C from cold. Prick the pastry base with a fork, then line with a large piece of greaseproof paper or crumpled foil to make it easier to handle. Fill with ceramic baking beans or dried pulses and bake for 15–20 minutes until the case looks 'set' but not at all coloured.

4 Carefully remove the paper or foil and the beans from the 'set' pastry case, then brush the inside with a little beaten egg to form a seal and prevent any leaks. Place back in the oven for a further 5–10 minutes until the base is firm to the touch and the sides are lightly coloured.

5 Reduce the oven temperature to 170°C/325°F/Gas 3; fan oven 150°C. Heat a frying pan and lightly fry the bacon until it is beginning to crisp and some of the fat has run out. Drain on kitchen paper and then spread it out evenly over the cooked pastry base. Place the eggs and yolks in a bowl and whisk together until combined. Beat in the cream and chives (if using), then season generously and add the nutmeg. Pour into the pastry case and bake for 35–40 minutes until just set and lightly golden. Serve hot or cold, cut into slices, with green salad.

33 Roast Loin of Pork with Apple Sauce

No. 9 BEST OF BRITISH

SERVES 8–10

2.25 kg/5 lb pork loin on the bone, skin lightly scored at 5-mm/ ¼-in intervals

2 tbsp cider vinegar

1 tbsp olive oil

2 tbsp coarse sea salt

8 fresh bay leaves

8 garlic cloves, unpeeled

3 fresh sage leaves

1 red onion, cut into wedges

1 glass red wine, about 120 ml/4 fl oz in total

600 ml/1 pint fresh chicken stock (from a carton is fine)

salt and freshly ground black pepper

roasted root vegetables and *Perfect Roast Potatoes* (p. 116), to serve

FOR THE APPLE SAUCE:

900 g/2 lb Bramley cooking apples, peeled, cored and sliced

juice of ¹/₂ lemon

1 tbsp caster sugar

50 g/2 oz unsalted butter, cut into cubes

To get a really good crackling, take a tip from the Chinese and pour boiling water just over the rind, leave for about 30 seconds, then repeat another couple of times. Don't be tempted to baste during cooking, and if the rind still hasn't crackled by the time the pork is cooked, remove it as described below and place under a hot grill to crisp.

1 Place the pork, skin-side down, on a chopping board and trim any loose fat or connective tissue into shape. Put in a roasting tin, then place in the sink, pour a kettle of boiling water over the pork rind and leave for 30 seconds. Repeat two or three times. Pour over the cider vinegar and massage into the skin to help dry out the rind. Transfer to a plate and leave uncovered in the fridge overnight.

2 Preheat the oven to 220°C/425°F/Gas 7; fan oven 200°C from cold. Place the pork joint in a roasting tin and drizzle over the oil, massaging it into the skin. Sprinkle over the sea salt and roast for 30 minutes, then reduce the oven temperature to 190°C/375°F/Gas 5; fan oven 170°C. Continue to cook for another 30 minutes, then add the bay leaves, garlic, sage and onion wedges, tossing to coat them in the juices. Cook for a further hour or until the pork is completely tender and the crackling is crispy. Nowadays it is perfectly safe to serve pork a little pink.

3 Meanwhile, make the apple sauce. Place the apples in a pan with 4–5 tablespoons cold water and the lemon juice. Cook over low heat for 12–15 minutes until the apples have softened, stirring occasionally. Stir in the sugar and whisk in the cubes of butter, then remove from the heat and keep warm. If you'd prefer a cold apple sauce, omit the butter. Spoon into a small bowl to serve.

4 When cooked, transfer the pork to a large platter and leave to rest in a warm place for 10–15 minutes. Place the roasting tin directly on the hob and deglaze the pan with the wine, scraping the bottom with a spoon to remove any sediment. Pour in the stock, increase the heat and simmer until the liquid has reduced by half. Season to taste, strain into a gravy boat and skim off any excess fat.

5 Cut through the fat of the rested joint just underneath the crackling to remove it in one piece, then cut into portions. Carve the pork into slices and arrange on serving plates with the roasted root vegetables and roast potatoes. Pass around the gravy and apple sauce separately to serve.

34 Toad in the Sky

SERVES 4

450 g/1 lb pork sausages (good quality)

1 tbsp beef dripping or olive oil

1 onion, roughly chopped

1 heaped tsp finely chopped fresh or 1/2 tsp dried sage

1 tbsp wholegrain mustard

300 ml/1/2 pint milk

50 g/2 oz unsalted butter, plus extra for greasing

100 g/4 oz plain flour, sifted

4 large eggs (preferably free-range or organic), separated

salt and freshly ground black pepper

baked beans, to serve (optional)

A twist on toad in the hole, except the sausages are reaching for the sky! I discovered this recipe in a 1960s newspaper and it works brilliantly. Nice use of your favourite pork sausages (I use Duchy of Cornwall or Musks) – just be sure to brown them first for that wonderful colour and flavour. It's really just a variation on a gougère, but my kids love it with baked beans and I can't argue with that; I like to season mine with black pepper and a large knob of butter.

1 Pan-fry the sausages in a non-stick frying pan over a fierce heat to brown them all over.

2 Heat the dripping or oil in a frying pan. Add the onion and cook for about 5 minutes until softened but not brown, stirring occasionally. Remove from the heat and fold in the sage, sausages and mustard until well combined.

3 Place the milk in a large pan with the butter and bring to the boil, stirring until the butter has melted. Tip in all of the flour, remove from the heat and beat vigorously until smooth and the mixture leaves the sides of the pan to form a 'ball'; do not over-beat. Season generously and leave to cool for 1–2 minutes.

4 Beat in the egg yolks, one at a time, until smooth and shiny. Place the egg whites in a bowl and beat until stiff but not dry, then fold a third into the batter to slacken. Carefully fold in the remaining egg whites until just combined.

5 Pour a third of the batter into a well-buttered 23–25-cm/9–10-in soufflé dish. Arrange the sausage mixture on top. Carefully pour over the remaining batter and smooth over the top with a palette knife. Bake near the top of the oven for about 40 minutes until well risen and golden brown. Serve at once with the baked beans, if liked.

35 Rabbit with Rosemary

SERVES 4

120 ml/4 fl oz olive oil

2 leeks, finely chopped

2 carrots, chopped

2 celery sticks, chopped

2 fresh bay leaves

4 dried red chillies

1.5 kg/3 lb rabbit, jointed, or 8 hind legs, well trimmed

175 g/6 oz pancetta or streaky bacon lardons

6 garlic cloves, peeled

1 tsp ground allspice

25 g/1 oz plain flour

450 ml/3/4 pint red wine

300 ml/1/2 pint fresh chicken stock (from a carton is fine)

2 tbsp chopped fresh rosemary

salt and freshly ground black pepper

mashed potatoes and buttered peas, to serve

Use farmed or wild rabbit; wild is excellent in dishes like this or for terrines, otherwise it tends to be too tough and a little dry. Rabbit has white flesh, is very tender and is low in fat, but unfortunately has become quite expensive recently, although it doesn't seem that long since it was cheaper than chicken – try it as a change. This is an adaptation of a Mediterranean recipe and is a delicious way of keeping the rabbit moist and full of flavour.

1 Place the oil, leeks, carrots, celery, bay leaves and chillies in a non-metallic bowl. Add the rabbit and season generously, then mix to combine. Cover with cling film and leave to marinate in the fridge for at least 2 hours (up to 24 hours is best), stirring a couple of times.

2 Heat a large, heavy-based, flameproof casserole dish. Remove the rabbit from the marinade, brushing off the vegetables, and add to the casserole in batches. Fry for about 10 minutes until nicely browned, turning regularly. Transfer to a plate.

3 Remove the bay leaves from the marinade and reserve, then remove and discard the chillies. Add the pancetta or bacon to the same casserole dish and, when it renders a little fat, add all the marinated vegetable mixture and the garlic. Cook for about 10 minutes until lightly golden and just tender, stirring.

4 Stir the allspice and flour into the casserole and cook for a minute or two, being careful not to let the flour catch on the bottom. Gradually pour in the wine, stirring constantly, then turn up the heat and boil for a few moments. Pour in the stock, stirring to combine, then turn down the heat and add the browned rabbit pieces, reserved bay leaves and the rosemary. Cover and simmer for about 45 minutes until the rabbit is completely tender. Season to taste. Serve straight from the casserole dish with bowls of the mashed potatoes and peas.

36 Faggots with Onion Gravy

SERVES 4–6

25 g/1 oz unsalted butter

1 onion, finely chopped

175 g/6 oz pigs' liver

2 pigs' hearts, trimmed and cut into chunks

450 g/1 lb pork belly, rind removed and roughly chopped

$^1/_2$ tsp ground mace

4 tbsp snipped fresh chives

1 tsp chopped fresh sage

1 egg (preferably free-range or organic), beaten

100 g/4 oz fresh white breadcrumbs

25 g/1 oz beef dripping or 3 tbsp olive oil

salt and freshly ground black pepper

mashed potatoes, to serve

FOR THE GRAVY:

4 red onions, each cut into 8 wedges

4 fresh thyme sprigs

1 tbsp olive oil

900 ml/1$^1/_2$ pints fresh beef stock (from a carton is fine)

300 ml/$^1/_2$ pint red wine

Pork is such a fantastic meat and one of the cheapest pound for pound. It is sadly under-used in this country. The French know how to use the pig. Nothing is waste – head, trotters, tail, ear, guts the whole lot is used for making many classic dishes. Well, here's a great British dish that does just that. It really is very easy to make and is well worth the effort. If you do not have a mincer at home, ask your butcher to mince all your meat for you.

1 Melt the butter in a small pan and add the onion, then cook for 3–4 minutes until softened and transparent, stirring occasionally. Leave to cool slightly.

2 Place a large bowl under the blade of a mincer which has been set up with the fine blade. Mince the pigs' liver, hearts and pork belly straight into the bowl. Add the cooled onions, the mace, chives, sage, egg and seasoning. Stir in the bread-crumbs, mixing to combine. Using your hands, shape into twelve even-sized patties, then place on a plate, cover with cling film and chill for about 1 hour to allow the mixture to firm up.

3 Preheat the oven to 200°C/400°F/Gas 6; fan oven 180°C from cold. To make the gravy, place the onion wedges in a large roasting tin. Add the thyme and drizzle with oil. Roast for 35–40 minutes until the onions are caramelized, tossing occa-sionally. Place the stock and wine in a pan, bring to the boil and reduce by a third.

4 Meanwhile, heat the dripping or oil in a large frying pan. Fry the faggots for 6–8 minutes until golden brown, turning once. Remove the roasted onions from the oven and arrange the faggots on top. Pour over the reduced stock mixture.

5 Reduce the oven temperature to 180°C/350°F/Gas 4; fan oven 160°C. Roast the faggots for 40 minutes or until completely tender and cooked through, basting occasionally. Arrange two to three faggots on each serving plate with some mashed potatoes. Spoon the onions over the faggots and pour over some of the gravy to serve.

37 Toad in the Hole

No. 7 BEST OF BRITISH

SERVES 4

100 g/4 oz plain flour

4 large eggs (preferably free-range or organic)

300 ml/¹/₂ pint milk

2 tbsp fresh thyme leaves

8 pork sausages (good-quality)

2 tbsp Dijon mustard

2 tbsp beef dripping or sunflower oil

salt and freshly ground black pepper

baked beans, to serve

Originally this classic English dish was made with rump steak or lamb chops, then it became a way of using up the Sunday roast leftovers, and subsequently we moved on to pork sausages, which were introduced as a willing partner for the Yorkshire pudding batter. The secret of a good toad in the hole is, of course, in the batter: mixing it quickly and giving it time to rest. It is also very important to heat the dripping or oil until very hot before pouring in the batter.

1 To make the batter, sift the flour into a large bowl with a good pinch of salt and a little pepper. Make a well in the centre and break in the eggs. Gradually draw in the flour with a wooden spoon and then slowly beat in the milk until the batter is the consistency of double cream. Strain through a sieve into a large jug to remove any lumps and stir in the thyme. Cover with plastic film and chill for at least 30 minutes, or ideally up to 3–4 hours.

2 Preheat the oven to 200°C/400°F/Gas 6; fan oven 180°C from cold. Heat a large non-stick frying pan and cook the sausages for about 5 minutes until golden brown, turning occasionally. If you do not have a non-stick pan, you'll need to add a little oil. Transfer to a plate and brush with the mustard.

3 Place the dripping or sunflower oil in a small roasting tray or ovenproof dish and pop into the oven for 5 minutes until the dripping is hot and hazy. Add the sausages to the hot tin and quickly pour in the batter. Immediately return the dish to the oven and cook for 35–40 minutes until the batter is well-risen and golden brown. Serve straight from the roasting tray with a bowl of baked beans.

38 Venison Chilli

225 g/8 oz dried red kidney beans, soaked overnight

2 tbsp olive oil

4 onions, finely chopped

4 garlic cloves, finely chopped

2 celery sticks, diced

2 red chillies, seeded and finely chopped

225 g/8 oz streaky bacon lardons

1 tbsp each ground cumin and paprika

1 heaped tsp each ground coriander, fennel seeds, cayenne pepper and ground black pepper

$1/2$ tsp ground cinnamon

1 tbsp chopped fresh oregano

1 kg/2$1/4$ lb coarsely minced venison

2 tsp unsweetened cocoa powder (optional)

2 x 400 g/14 oz cans chopped tomatoes

2 heaped tbsp tomato purée

1 fresh bay leaf

1.2 litres/2 pints chicken or vegetable stock (from a carton is fine)

salt

bowls of chopped red onion, guacamole, taco chips and crème fraîche, to serve

There are so many different recipes for chilli, and so many differing opinions as to the correct version. Well, I've spent a good deal of time developing this recipe and it's pretty damn good. Perfect for feeding crowd or a wonderful freezer standby for nights when you're craving a spicy TV supper dish. If venison mince is hard to find (use a reputable butcher rather than a supermarket), you can substitute a mixture of coarsely ground pork and beef.

1 Drain the beans, place in a pan with plenty of boiling water and boil fast for 15 minutes. Drain, rinse well, put them back into the pan with fresh water and simmer for 1 hour until tender, topping up with boiling water as necessary. Drain and rinse briefly.

2 Heat the oil in a large pan, add the onions, garlic, celery and chillies and cook for 15 minutes until softened and lightly golden, stirring occasionally. Add the bacon and cook for another 10–15 minutes until the bacon is sizzling and golden, stirring. Stir in the spices and the oregano and continue to cook for 1–2 minutes, stirring.

3 Add the venison and cook for 10–15 minutes, stirring until browned, then stir in the cocoa (if using) with the kidney beans, tomatoes, tomato purée, bay leaf and 900 ml/1$1/2$ pints of the stock. Bring to the boil, season with salt to taste and then reduce the heat and simmer for 2–2$1/2$ hours, adding the remaining stock as necessary, until the venison is completely tender but still covered with juice. Transfer the chilli to a large serving dish and serve hot with bowls of chopped red onion, guacamole, taco chips and crème fraîche or soured cream.

39 Thai Chicken Curry

SERVES 4

50 g/2 oz bunch fresh coriander

5 shallots, chopped

2 garlic cloves, chopped

2 tbsp sunflower oil

2 tbsp Thai green curry paste

2 x 400 g/14 oz cans coconut milk

250 ml/8 fl oz fresh chicken stock (from a carton is fine)

12 skinless, boneless chicken thighs, cut into bite-sized pieces

2 tbsp Thai fish sauce (nam pla) or light soy sauce

grated rind and juice of 1 lime

1 tbsp caster sugar

good handful fresh basil leaves, roughly torn

salt and freshly ground black pepper

Thai fragrant rice and lime wedges, to serve

I am really into the smooth, silky taste of this very easy curry. Green curry paste is now available in all supermarkets, but very good-quality ones can be found in Oriental supermarkets or Asian stores. If you're really keen I suppose you could always make your own, but I never usually bother. I like to serve my Thai curries with Thai fragrant rice. The long white grains have a characteristically soft and slightly sticky texture when cooked. You'll need to allow approximately 50 g/2 oz rice per person.

1 Remove a good handful of the coriander leaves from the stalks – about a quarter – and reserve. Roughly chop the remainder, including the stalks, and place in a mini-blender with the shallots and garlic. Whizz to a paste.

2 Heat a wok or heavy-based frying pan. Add the oil and stir-fry the curry paste for 1 minute over a high heat. Add 150 ml/$\frac{1}{4}$ pint of the coconut milk and the coriander paste, stirring well to combine. Cook for 2 minutes, then add the chicken stock and boil for 8–10 minutes until the natural oils start to appear on the surface, stirring occasionally. Season generously.

3 Stir in the chicken, reduce the heat and simmer for 15 minutes until the chicken is completely tender and the sauce has reduced considerably with the oils clearly visible on the surface.

4 Add the remaining coconut milk, the fish sauce or soy sauce, lime rind and juice and sugar, bring to a simmer and cook for another 5 minutes. Add the reserved coriander leaves and the basil and cook for another minute or two. Serve hot with bowls of the rice and lime wedges.

40 Chicken Kiev

SERVES 4

4 x 225 g/8 oz skinless chicken breasts

sunflower or vegetable oil, for deep-frying

salt and freshly ground black pepper

herbed rice, to serve

FOR THE GARLIC HERB BUTTER:

3-4 tbsp chopped fresh flatleaf parsley

3-4 tbsp snipped fresh chives

1 tsp chopped fresh tarragon

100 g/4 oz unsalted butter, softened

2 garlic cloves, crushed to a paste wih a little sea salt

3/4 tsp prepared English mustard

FOR THE KIEV COATING:

175 g/6 oz toasted natural breadcrumbs

25 g/1 oz freshly grated Parmesan cheese

4 eggs, beaten (preferably free-range or organic)

50 g/2 oz plain flour

One of those dishes that never seems to fade in popularity – a classic 1960s number, still going strong. The Italians call it *pollo sorpresa*. During cooking the butter melts within the chicken, creating a vacuum, so unless you allow the chicken to rest for a couple of minutes before serving, your guests may end up wearing most of the butter down the front of their clothes!

1 To prepare the garlic herb butter, place the herbs in a bowl and add the softened butter. Add the garlic to the butter mixture with the mustard and a good grinding of pepper, then mix together with a fork to combine.

2 Divide the butter into four sections, then plunge your hands into a bowl of cold water before moulding each piece into a torpedo shape. Roll each one in grease-proof paper, twisting the ends to secure. Chill for at least 30 minutes to allow the butter to harden.

3 Place the chicken breasts on a chopping board. Remove the fillet from under-neath each one and set aside. Make a vertical cut down the length of each chicken breast, but not all the way through. Place the breasts between cling film and bash with a rolling pin to ensure an even fillet – this will help stop any garlic butter from leaking out of the chicken. Repeat with the small fillets. Unwrap the chilled garlic herb butter pieces and place one piece down the centre of each breast, then place the small fillets on top, pushing down to seal.

4 Place the breadcrumbs and Parmesan in a shallow dish, season and mix well. Break the eggs into a separate shallow dish and lightly whisk to combine. Put the flour on a flat plate and season generously. Dust the chicken breasts in the seasoned flour, then dip into the beaten egg and finally roll in the breadcrumb mixture, making sure at each stage that each breast is well coated. Arrange on a baking sheet, cover with cling film and chill for at least 30 minutes (up to 24 hours is fine).

5 Heat the oil in a deep-fat fryer to 180°C/350°F. Add the coated chicken breasts and fry for 8–10 minutes until cooked through and golden brown. Drain well on kitchen paper and allow to rest for a minute or two, then arrange on serving plates and serve immediately with the herbed rice.

41 Chicken Stir-fry with Black Beans

SERVES 4

1 egg white

$1/2$ tsp salt

5 tsp cornflour

450 g/1 lb skinless chicken fillets, cut into 2.5-cm/1-in pieces

2 tbsp groundnut oil

4 garlic cloves, finely chopped

5-cm/2-in piece fresh root ginger, peeled and finely chopped

$1/2$ tsp dried red chilli flakes

2 tbsp finely chopped Chinese black beans, fermented or salted

2 carrots, sliced on the diagonal

1 red pepper, seeded and cut into diamonds

1 yellow pepper, seeded and cut into diamonds

175 ml/6 fl oz fresh chicken stock (from a carton is fine)

2 tbsp dark soy sauce

3 tbsp rice vinegar

pinch sugar

175 g/6 oz sugar snap peas

4 spring onions, sliced on the diagonal

steamed rice, to serve

A classic Chinese restaurant dish, simple, with lovely tastes and textures, and plenty of crunchy vegetables that are good for you. It makes a robust partner for some plain boiled rice, but be warned: everyone will be back for second helpings. The secret is in a traditional Oriental technique called velveting which makes the chicken meltingly tender. I always eat this dish at Chinese restaurants, but it is also easy to make at home.

1 Lightly beat the egg white in a non-metallic bowl with the salt and 2 teaspoons of the cornflour. Add the chicken, cover with cling film and chill for 30 minutes.

2 Place 300 ml/$1/2$ pint water in a pan and bring to the boil. Stir the chicken, then remove from the marinade, wiping off any excess liquid, and add to the pan of water, stirring to prevent it from sticking, then return to the heat and cook for $1 1/2$ minutes or until the chicken is white and just tender. Drain on kitchen paper.

3 Heat a wok and swirl in the oil. Add the garlic, ginger, chilli flakes and black beans and stir-fry for 15 seconds, then add the carrots and stir-fry for 1 minute. Stir in the cooked chicken and the peppers. Pour in the stock and add the soy sauce, vinegar and sugar, stirring to combine.

4 Increase the heat and bring to the boil, then reduce to a simmer, add the sugar snap peas and spring onions and cook for 3 minutes until tender. Mix the remaining cornflour with $1 1/2$ tablespoons water and stir into the wok. Cook for a minute or so until the sauce clears and thickens. Serve at once in Chinese-style bowls with the rice.

42 Roast Turkey with Spiced Rub

SERVES 18–20

1 head garlic, cloves separated but not peeled, about 75 g/ 3 oz in total

olive oil, for drizzling

3 tbsp caraway seeds

1 tbsp cumin seeds

4 tbsp sea salt, plus extra for seasoning

2 tbsp dried oregano

1 tbsp finely chopped fresh rosemary

3 tbsp ground black pepper, plus extra for seasoning

1^1/$_2$ tsp ground turmeric

6 tbsp harissa or chilli sauce

6.5 kg/14 lb oven-ready turkey, at room temperature (preferably Kelly Bronze)

about 40 g/1^1/$_2$ oz unsalted butter, for greasing

2 tbsp plain flour

150 ml/^{1}/$_4$ pint red wine

about 300 ml/^{1}/$_2$ pint fresh turkey or chicken stock (from a carton is fine)

Perfect Roast Potatoes (p. 116), *Corn Pudding* (p. 74), seasonal vegetables and cranberry relish, to serve

Christmas Day always seems to create a modicum of panic. However, all it takes is careful planning, which is why this recipe works so well as it needs to be prepared a day in advance.

1 Preheat the oven to 200°C/400°F/Gas 6; fan oven 180°C from cold. Place the garlic cloves in a small roasting tin and drizzle over a little oil. Roast for 15 minutes until completely tender. Remove from the oven and set aside until they are cool enough to handle, then push the roasted garlic pulp out of the skin, using the back of a knife – you'll need 3 tablespoons of pulp in total.

2 Heat a heavy-based frying pan and roast the caraway and cumin seeds for a few minutes until aromatic. Place in a mini blender or coffee grinder with the salt, oregano, rosemary, pepper and turmeric. Grind to a powder and then tip into a bowl. Add the garlic pulp and harissa or chilli sauce and mix well to combine. Using both hands, rub the mixture all over the skin of the turkey and into the cavity. Cover with cling film and leave to marinate at room temperature for 1–2 hours, or preferably up to 24 hours in the fridge or in a cool place.

3 Preheat the oven to 230°C/450°F/Gas 8; fan oven 210°C from cold. Lay a large sheet of foil lengthways over a large roasting tin, leaving enough at each end to wrap over the turkey, then lightly butter the foil. Repeat this exercise with another sheet of foil, this time across the tin. Lightly butter once again. Place the marinated turkey breast-side up in the centre of the foil, then wrap to enclose.

4 Place the turkey in the oven and roast for 30 minutes, then reduce the oven temperature to 200°C/400°F/Gas 6; fan oven 180°C . Roast for another 2^1/$_2$ hours. About 30 minutes before the end of the estimated cooking time, fold back the foil, baste the bird well and return to the oven until cooked – just make sure that the ends of the drumsticks are still covered or they may burn. The turkey should be a rich, dark brown colour. To be sure that it is cooked, either insert a meat thermometer into the thickest part of the thigh to check the temperature, or insert a fine skewer into the thickest part of the thigh: the juices should run clear, but if they are still pink, return the bird to the oven, laying a fresh sheet of foil

contd. overleaf

over it once it is well browned. Check again every 15 minutes until you are happy that the turkey is cooked right the way through, then remove it from the oven.

5 Lift the cooked turkey on to a serving platter, cover and leave to rest in a warm place for the juices to settle and to ease carving. Skim all the fat from the cooking juices and then stir the flour into the tin's residue. Cook on the hob over a low heat for a minute or so, stirring until golden. Gradually pour in the wine and stock, stirring all the time until smooth after each addition. Bring to the boil and let bubble for 2–3 minutes until thickened. Season to taste. Carve the turkey into slices and arrange on serving plates with some of the gravy, the potatoes, *Corn Pudding*, a selection of seasonal vegetables and cranberry relish.

43 Corn Pudding

SERVES 6–8

25 g/1 oz unsalted butter, plus a little extra for greasing

100 g/4 oz streaky bacon lardons

450 g/1 lb leeks, trimmed and shredded

1 red pepper, seeded and diced

3 corn cobs, blanched and nibs removed, or 350 g/12 oz frozen sweetcorn, thawed and well drained

2 tbsp chopped fresh flatleaf parsley

3 egg yolks (preferably free-range or organic)

1 tsp prepared English mustard

600 ml/1 pint double cream

4 drops Tabasco sauce

splash Worcestershire sauce

salt and freshly ground pepper

This pudding has an American influence as I first came across a version of it at a Thanksgiving dinner. Serve it at Christmas with your *Roast Turkey with Spiced Rub* (p. 73-74). It also makes an excellent filling for quiche or can be served cold with sliced meats and salads. It can be prepared in advance and simply reheated in a low oven for about 30 minutes before serving.

1 Preheat the oven to 180°C/350°F/Gas 4; fan oven 160°C from cold. Melt the butter in a large pan and add the bacon. Cook for 2–3 minutes until crispy, stirring occasionally. Add the leeks and red pepper and continue to cook for another 5 minutes until softened, stirring occasionally. Season to taste. Add the sweetcorn and parsley and mix well to combine, then quickly cook out any excess liquid. Tip into a buttered 23–25-cm/9–10-in soufflé dish and level the top.

2 Place the egg yolks in a bowl with the mustard and cream. Whisk together and then add the Tabasco and Worcestershire sauces. Season to taste. Pour this over the sweetcorn mixture and bake for 45–50 minutes until lightly golden and just set. Serve hot.

44 Tea-smoked Barbary Duck

SERVES 4

4 x 225 g/8 oz Barbary duck breasts, well trimmed

4 tsp sesame oil

50 g/2 oz jasmine tea

50 g/2 oz light muscovado sugar

50 g/2 oz long-grain rice

1 tbsp hoisin sauce

1 tsp katchup manis (sweet soy sauce, also known as kecap manis)

spring onion and red chilli shreds and fresh coriander sprigs, to garnish

Thai fragrant rice and *Greens with Oyster Sauce* (p. 114), to serve

The Barbary duck is far less fatty than the traditional English duck that we are used to and is perfect for this dish. Jasmine tea is black or green tea that has been mixed with the dried flowers of the scented white jasmine.

1 Lightly score the skin of each duck breast in a lattice pattern with a small, sharp knife. Using a pastry brush, brush each one all over with 1 teaspoon of the sesame oil, then arrange them on a rack that will fit into a wok with a lid. Cut out a small circle of foil about 20 cm/8 in diameter. Scrunch the sides until you have a container of about 13 cm/5 in diameter. Mix together the tea, sugar and rice in a bowl, pour into the container and place it in the bottom of the wok. Place on the hob.

2 Turn up the heat to full and, once the tea starts smoking, add the rack with the duck breasts on top. Cover with the lid and leave the heat on for 10 minutes. Don't be tempted to look under the lid as the smoke will disperse and stop the duck from cooking. Remove the wok from the heat and still don't lift the lid. Allow the wok to cool for 5 minutes and the smoke slowly to dissipate, then remove the duck breasts, transfer to a plate and allow to cool completely. The duck is now smoked and just needs a final cooking. It will keep at this stage for at least 24 hours covered with cling film in the fridge.

3 Preheat the oven to 200°C/400°F/Gas 6; fan oven 180°C from cold. Heat a large, ovenproof frying-pan over a moderate heat. When the pan is hot, add the duck breasts, fat-side down, and cook for 1–2 minutes until the skin is golden.

4 Mix together the hoisin sauce and katchup manis in a small bowl. Remove the duck from the heat and drain off all the excess fat. Using a pastry brush, brush the fillet side of each duck breast with 1 teaspoon of the hoisin mixture, then turn the duck fillets over so that they are facing skin-side up. Transfer to the oven and cook for another 5–6 minutes if you like your duck pink, a few more minutes if you don't.

5 Remove the duck from the oven and leave rest for a couple of minutes, then carve each breast on the diagonal and fan out on to hot serving plates. Add a portion of the Thai fragrant rice (moulding this in a dariole looks good) and a small mound of the greens on to each plate and scatter the spring onion and chilli shreds over the rice. Garnish each duck breast with a coriander sprig to serve.

45 Hot Chilli Chicken Fajitas

SERVES 4

2 tbsp chilli oil

1 tbsp hot chilli powder

1 tbsp paprika

pinch caster sugar

grated rind and juice of 1 lime

4 skinless chicken breast fillets

8 soft flour tortillas

1 small iceberg lettuce, shredded

150 ml/¼ pint soured cream

FOR THE TOMATO AND AVOCADO SALSA:

4 large tomatoes, seeded and finely diced

1 red chilli, seeded and finely chopped

juice of 1 lime

1 small red onion, finely chopped

2 ripe avocados, peeled, stoned and finely diced

2 tbsp olive oil

8 tbsp roughly chopped fresh coriander

salt and freshly ground black pepper

I always keep a packet of flour tortillas in the cupboard – they often come in handy. To make them soft enough for rolling, pop them on a hot frying or griddle pan, or alternatively microwave on high between dampened sheets of kitchen paper for about 30 seconds. The longer the chicken is left to 'sleep' in the chilli mixture, the better it tastes, then it just needs to be slapped on the chargrill for a couple of minutes on each side.

1 Soak 8 x 15-cm/6-in bamboo skewers in water overnight. Mix together the chilli oil, chilli powder, paprika, sugar and lime rind and juice in a shallow, non-metallic dish. Cut each chicken breast lengthways into six strips. Add to the chilli mixture and stir until well coated, then cover with cling film and leave to marinate in the fridge for 1–2 hours.

2 To make the tomato and avocado salsa, place all the ingredients into a large bowl and stir gently to combine. Season to taste and spoon into a serving bowl. Cover with cling film and set aside to allow the flavours to develop – don't make this too far in advance or the avocados are in danger of going black.

3 Heat a griddle pan or a barbecue. Thread three pieces of chicken on to each soaked bamboo skewer and place on the griddle pan or barbecue. Cook for 3–4 minutes on each side until the chicken is cooked through and lightly charred.

4 Heat a frying or griddle pan. Add a soft flour tortilla and heat for 30 seconds (turning once) or until soft and pliable. Repeat with the remaining flour tortillas and stack up on a warmed plate. Place the chicken skewers on a serving platter and hand around the tomato and avocado salsa, warmed tortillas, the lettuce and soured cream, allowing each person to assemble the fajitas themselves.

46 Salt-crust Roast Chicken

1 small onion, quartered

1/2 lemon, cut into wedges

few fresh rosemary branches or fresh thyme sprigs

4 garlic cloves, peeled

1.5–1.75 kg/3–4 lb oven-ready chicken (preferably free-range or organic)

melted butter, for brushing

FOR THE SALT CRUST:

1 kg/2¹/4 lb plain flour, plus extra for dusting

750 g/1¹/2 lb coarse sea salt, plus 1 tbsp

3 egg whites, lightly beaten

1 egg yolk, beaten with 2 tbsp water

salt and freshly ground black pepper

buttered carrots, sprouting broccoli and *Perfect Roast Potatoes* (p. 116), to serve

There's nothing nicer than a good roast chicken. Mind you, the first thing you need is a really good bird, ideally free-range or, better still, if you have the spare cash, organic or a poulet de Bresse, the king of French chickens. This is a different way of roasting that is impressive and keeps the chicken juicy.

1 Preheat the oven to 180°C/350°F/Gas 4; fan oven 160°C from cold. To make the salt crust, place the flour in a large bowl with the 750 g (1¹/2 lb) sea salt and stir to combine. Make a hollow in the centre and add the egg whites, mixing to combine, and gradually add enough water to form a rough dough – you'll need no more than 600 ml/1 pint in total. Remove the dough from the bowl and place on a lightly floured work surface, then cover with cling film and leave to rest for 15 minutes.

2 Place the onion, lemon, rosemary or thyme and garlic in the body cavity of the chicken. Truss the bird with the wings folded under the body and the legs tied together. Weigh the chicken and calculate the cooking time, allowing 20 minutes per 450 g/1 lb, plus 20 minutes. Brush all over with melted butter and season with a little salt and plenty of pepper.

3 Knead the rested dough to form a smooth ball, adding flour as needed, then roll out on a lightly floured work surface to a 5-mm/1/4-in thickness. Place the chicken in the middle of the dough, breast-side down, and carefully fold over the dough to enclose, trimming off any excess. Turn the chicken back over into a large roasting tin and repair any small holes with the dough trimmings. You can also use the trimmings to decorate; or just lightly score to give a feathered effect. Lightly brush with the egg-yolk mixture to seal and sprinkle with the remaining tablespoon of sea salt.

4 Roast the chicken as calculated; you can keep an eye on how it is cooking by sticking a meat thermometer through the salt dough and into the thickest part of the thigh before cooking. Just make sure you seal back up around the edges where the thermometer has gone in. When the chicken is cooked, the crust will be rock-solid and golden brown. Remove it from the oven and leave to rest for 20 minutes. When you are ready to serve, break open the crust to find a deliciously moist, juicy chicken that is full of flavour. Discard the crust and carve the chicken into slices and serve with the carrots, broccoli and roast potatoes.

47 Butterflied Poussin

SERVES 4–6

1 tbsp Sichuan peppercorns
(optional)

4 poussins

3 tbsp finely chopped fresh
root ginger

4 large garlic cloves, finely
chopped, about 1 tbsp in total

grated rind of 3 large oranges,
about 4 tbsp in total

4 spring onions, finely chopped

1 red chilli, seeded and finely
chopped

2 tbsp clear honey

2 tbsp dark soy sauce

450 ml/³/₄ pint corn oil

120 ml/4 fl oz sesame oil

2 tbsp chopped fresh coriander

salt and freshly ground black
pepper

Saffron Pilaff (p. 115) and
green salad, to serve

Poussins are the smallest chickens available to buy. I like them
because they are very tender and quick to cook. Sometimes you can
now buy them in selected supermarkets already spatchcocked. You
can sieve the marinade before basting the poussins during cooking.
This helps stop uneven browning, but I usually don't bother.

1 Place the Sichuan peppercorns (if using) in a small frying pan, if using, and toast
for a few minutes until aromatic, tossing occasionally, then grind to a powder in a
mini-blender, coffee grinder or pestle and mortar. Set aside.

2 Using poultry shears or sharp kitchen scissors, cut each poussin along the back,
down each side of the backbone, then remove and discard the backbone. Snip
the wishbone in half and open out the poussin, then snip out the ribs. Turn over,
so it is skin-side up, and press down firmly on the breastbone with the heel of
your hand to flatten it out. Trim off any excess skin, wash under cold running
water and pat dry with kitchen paper.

3 Place the ginger in a mini-blender or pestle and mortar with the ground Sichuan
pepper (if using) the garlic, orange rind, spring onions and chilli and blitz or
pound to a smooth paste. Transfer to a large, plastic container with a lid and add
the honey, soy sauce, corn oil and sesame oil. Season to taste and stir until well
combined. Add the butterflied poussins and turn to coat, then secure the lid and
leave to marinate in the fridge for at least 4 hours or preferably overnight, shaking
the container occasionally.

4 When you are ready to cook, preheat either the grill to medium-hot or the oven
to 220°C/425°F/Gas 7; fan oven 200°C from cold. Thread 2 x 22-cm/9-in thick
metal skewers in a criss-cross fashion through each butterflied poussin, wiping off
any excess marinade. This will hold and keep them flat during cooking and also
makes them much easier to handle – just don't forget your oven gloves!

5 Arrange the poussins on the wire rack of a grill pan or on a wire rack in a large
roasting tin, skin-side up, and cook for 10–15 minutes on each side until golden
brown and just tender, basting occasionally. Leave to rest in a warm place for a
couple of minutes, then remove the skewers and sprinkle over the coriander.
Serve at once with the pilaff and salad.

48 Paella

No. 1   HOLIDAY DISHES

SERVES 6-8

1.2 litres/2 pints fresh chicken stock (from a carton is fine)

1/2 tsp saffron strands, soaked in a little warm water

about 120 ml/4 fl oz olive oil

175 g/6 oz chorizo, sliced

100 g/4 oz pancetta, diced

8 skinless, boneless chicken thighs, halved

2 garlic cloves, finely chopped

1 large Spanish onion, diced

1 red pepper, seeded and diced

1 tsp fresh soft thyme leaves

1/2 tsp dried red chilli flakes

600 ml/1 pint Spanish short-grain rice (calasparra)

1 tsp paprika

120 m/1/4 fl oz dry white wine

100 g/4 oz podded fresh or frozen peas

4 large tomatoes, peeled

18 small clams, cleaned

12 raw jumbo prawns, shells intact

450 g/1 lb squid in 1 in dice

5 tbsp chopped fresh flatleaf parsley, to garnish

salt and freshly ground pepper

A Spanish rice dish, originating in Valencia, and the name actually refers to the cooking vessel, a paellera. There are hundreds of versions of this dish, each household and restaurant having its own. This is one-pot dining at its best, and could include anything you fancy: rabbit, snails and green beans seem to have been the original constituents with, of course, Spanish short-grained rice and saffron. Have fun playing with your own combinations.

1 Heat the stock and saffron in a pan to boiling point. Heat half the oil in a paella dish or large, heavy-based sauté pan. Add the chorizo and pancetta and fry for a few minutes until crisp and lightly golden, then transfer to a plate and set aside. Add the chicken pieces to the pan and fry for a few minutes on each side until golden; remove and set aside with the chorizo and pancetta.

2 Add half the remaining olive oil to the pan. Add the finely chopped garlic, the onion and red pepper and continue to cook for another few minutes until the vegetables have softened but not coloured, stirring occasionally.

3 Add the thyme to the pan with the chilli flakes and rice and stir for about 2 minutes or until all the grains of rice are nicely coated and glossy. Stir in the paprika, then pour in the wine and allow it to bubble down a little, stirring. Pour in the hot chicken stock, add the cooked chorizo, pancetta and chicken thighs and cook for about 5 minutes, stirring occasionally.

4 Seed and dice the tomatoes, fold them in with the peas and season to taste. Put in the clams with the edges that will open facing outwards and continue to cook gently for another 10–15 minutes or until the rice is just tender. Remove from the hob and leave to rest in a warm place for 10 minutes.

5 Meanwhile, heat the remaining oil in a separate large frying pan. Quickly tip in the prawns and stir-fry for a minute or two, then scatter the prawns over the paella. Add the squid to the pan and stir-fry for 1 minute or so until just tender, then scatter the squid over the paella, discarding the garlic. Garnish with the parsley and serve immediately, straight from the paella dish.

49 Pancetta-wrapped Chicken Parcels with Gorgonzola

SERVES 4

100 g/4 oz unsalted butter, at room temperature

150 g/5 oz Gorgonzola cheese

75 g/3 oz stale white breadcrumbs

1 heaped tsp fresh thyme leaves

2 tbsp chopped fresh flatleaf parsley

8 large, skinless, boneless chicken thighs, well trimmed

16 thin slices pancetta or 16 x 4-cm/1^1/$_2$-in slices prosciutto

2 tbsp olive oil

150 ml/^{1}/$_4$ pint double cream

175 g/6 oz Taleggio cheese, cut into small cubes

2 tbsp freshly grated Parmesan cheese

salt and freshly ground black pepper

plum tomato slices, red onion slivers, snipped fresh chives and balsamic dressing, plus green salad, to serve

If you're lucky enough to have any chicken parcels left over, they are fantastic cold and would make great picnic fare in the warmer months. Try them sliced in a gourmet sandwich, with lashings of the Taleggio cream, some sliced seedless black grapes and plenty of salad leaves on walnut or ciabatta bread. Taleggio is an unpasteurized, soft cow's cheese from northern Italy which is well worth seeking out. Most supermarkets now stock it, but you may find it in better condition in a specialist cheesemonger's or deli.

1 Preheat the oven to 200°C/400°F/Gas 6; fan oven 180°C from cold. To make the stuffing, place 75 g/3 oz of the butter, the Gorgonzola, breadcrumbs, thyme and parsley in a bowl and mix to combine. Divide into eight even-sized balls, then shape into cubes.

2 Open out each chicken thigh, place between two pieces of cling film and flatten out with a rolling pin. Add a grinding of black pepper to each one and place a cube of the stuffing in the middle. Fold over to enclose the filling completely, then wrap each one with two pieces of the pancetta or prosciutto. Secure each one with two cocktail sticks in a criss-cross fashion.

3 Heat a large, heavy-based frying pan. Add the oil and then the chicken parcels. Cook over a medium heat for a minute or so on each side to seal completely, then transfer to the oven and cook for another 15–20 minutes until the chicken is cooked through and tender.

4 Meanwhile, make the Taleggio cream. Melt the remaining butter in a small pan. Add the cream, Taleggio and Parmesan and season with pepper. Simmer gently for 3–4 minutes until the cheeses are melted, stirring occasionally. Keep warm over a low heat.

5 To serve, arrange the tomatoes in an overlapping layer around the edge of each serving plate. Scatter over the red onion and chives and season generously, then drizzle over a little of the balsamic dressing. Drizzle the Taleggio cream in a zigzag pattern in the middle of each plate. Remove the cocktail sticks from the chicken parcels and arrange two in the middle of each plate. Serve at once with green salad.

50 Smoked Haddock Fish Cakes

SERVES 4

350 g/12 oz potatoes, cut into chunks

4 eggs (preferably free-range or organic)

225 g/8 oz haddock fillet (in one piece)

175 g/6 oz undyed smoked haddock fillet (in one piece)

300 ml/1/2 pint milk

2 fresh bay leaves

few peppercorns

100 g/4 oz unsalted butter

1 small onion, finely chopped

2 tsp anchovy essence

2 tbsp chopped fresh flatleaf parsley

1 tbsp chopped fresh dill

25 g/1 oz seasoned plain flour

100 g/4 oz toasted natural breadcrumbs

salt and freshly ground black pepper

buttered spinach and *Classic Parsley Sauce* (p. 119), to serve

Whenever I put these perennial British favourites on the menu at my restaurant, they walk out the door. I usually serve them on a bed of buttered spinach surrounded by parsley sauce. Most customers want chips too – good for them. I use a mixture of fish for this recipe, but you could use just one variety and increase the quantity. Don't over-process the fish-cake mixture, as it's impressive to see chunks of fish when you cut the fish cake open.

1 Place the potatoes in a pan of boiling salted water, cover and cook for 15–20 minutes until tender. Drain and return to the pan for a couple of minutes to dry out, then mash well. Meanwhile cook 2 of the eggs in a small pan of simmering water for 10–12 minutes until hard-boiled. Rinse under cold water and crack away the shell, then finely chop.

2 Place the fish in a large sauté pan with the milk, bay leaves and peppercorns. Cover and bring to a simmer, then poach for a few minutes until the fish is just tender. Transfer the fish to a plate with a fish slice and flake, discarding any skin and bones. Strain the milk into a jug – you'll need 300 ml/1/2 pint if you want to make the Parsley sauce.

3 Heat 25 g/1 oz of the butter in a frying pan and sweat the onion for about 5 minutes until softened, then add another 25 g/1 oz of the butter and just allow to melt. Tip into a bowl and add the mashed potatoes, flaked fish, hard-boiled eggs, anchovy essence, parsley and dill, then mix well. Season, cover with cling film and chill for at least 1 hour (up to 24 hours is fine) to firm up.

4 Shape the fish mixture into four patties and then toss in the flour. Beat the remaining eggs in a shallow dish and add the patties, turning to coat, then coat in the breadcrumbs. Arrange on a baking sheet and chill for at least 2 hours to firm up. Heat the remaining butter in a frying pan and fry the patties for 5 minutes on each side until heated through and golden brown. Arrange the spinach on serving plates and place the fish cakes on top, then pour around some of the *Classic Parsley Sauce* to serve.

51 Bouillabaisse

No. 2 HOLIDAY DISHES

SERVES 6–8

5 tbsp olive oil

2 onions, finely chopped

6 garlic cloves, finely chopped

2 leeks, trimmed and finely chopped

1 fennel bulb, finely chopped (reserve the tops)

750 g/1½ lb ripe tomatoes, chopped

1 tsp fennel seeds

1 tsp tomato purée

1 small bunch fresh flatleaf parsley, separated into leaves and stalks

3 fresh thyme sprigs

2 fresh bay leaves

3 red mullet, scaled and filleted, heads and bones reserved

900 g/2 lb sea bass, scaled and filleted each fillet cut into 3 pieces, heads and bones reserved

12 large raw tiger prawns, peeled and veins removed, shells reserved

2 strips pared orange rind

600 ml/1 pint fresh fish stock (from a carton is fine)

2-litre/3½-pint bottle still mineral water

1 tsp saffron strands, soaked in a little warm water

2 tbsp Pernod liqueur

450 g/1 lb monkfish fillet, cut into 4-cm/1½-in chunks

1 kg/2½ 4 lb mussels, cleaned, about 36 in total

salt and freshly ground black pepper

First invented by the fishermen from Marseille as a fish stew which they would cook up on the boat, using all the small fish that most people would throw back. As it grew in popularity chefs picked up on the idea and started adding other fish and shellfish. Ideally it is made with a selection of Mediterranean fish (gurnard, rascasse and grey mullet), but these are rarely available in our fishmongers. It is a wonderful dish with a lovely combination of flavours, so experiment with whatever selection of fish you can get hold of.

1 Heat the oil in a large pan. Add the onions, garlic, leeks and fennel and cook gently for 10 minutes until the vegetables are soft but not coloured, stirring occasionally. Stir in the tomatoes, fennel seeds, tomato purée, parsley stalks, thyme and bay leaves, then add the reserved fish trimmings and prawn shells, stirring to coat. Cook for a minute or so, stirring until everything is well combined.

2 Add the orange rind and pour in the fish stock, mineral water and saffron mixture. Bring to the boil, reduce the heat and simmer gently, uncovered, for 25-30 minutes, skimming the surface occasionally to remove any froth.

3 When the fish broth has reduced to about 2 litres/3½ pints, remove from the heat and strain into a clean pan. Add the Pernod and season to taste. Return to a simmer, then add the sea bass and red mullet fillets with the monkfish, and mussels. Bring back up to a simmer and tip in the prawns. Cover and cook for another 2 minutes or until the mussels have opened and the prawns have turned pink. Using a slotted spoon, transfer the fish and shellfish to a warmed serving platter and pour the soup into a tureen. Roughly chop the parsley leaves and scatter on top to serve.

52 Seafood Laksa

SERVES 6

groundnut oil, for cooking

9 baby squid, cleaned and cut into 5-cm/2-in pieces

350 g/12 oz monkfish fillet, skinned and cut into 5-cm/2-in chunks

18 raw tiger prawns, peeled and veins removed

juice of 1 large lemon

2 medium-hot red chillies, halved and seeded

4 garlic cloves, roughly chopped

5 cm/2 in piece fresh root ginger, peeled and roughly chopped

1 tsp ground toasted coriander seeds

50 g/2 oz bunch fresh coriander (including roots)

50 ml/2 fl oz sesame oil

1.2 litres/2 pints coconut milk

900 ml/1½ pints fresh fish or vegetable stock (from a carton is fine)

200 g/7 oz dried vermicelli noodles

175 g/6 oz sugar snap peas

50 ml/2 fl oz Thai fish sauce (nam pla)

handful fresh mint and basil leaves

3 spring onions, thinly sliced

In Indonesia and Malaysia, laksa is the name of a rice noodle dish, usually with a creamy curry or tart tamarind sauce. You can now buy laksa paste in some supermarkets, but if you have the time, prepare your own, as it does make a world of difference. This is my personal version of the dish, and I do not claim authenticity. It is the ultimate one-pot noodle – a filling meal in itself or, served in tiny bowls, a wonderful starter. Traditionally it is garnished with laksa leaves, but I find that a mixture of mint and basil leaves produces the best flavour.

1 Heat a griddle pan. Brush with a little oil and then chargrill the squid for 30–45 seconds on each side. Transfer to a plate and leave to cool, then add the monkfish and prawns. Squeeze over the lemon juice and set aside to marinate.

2 Heat a large pan. Place the chillies in a food processor with the garlic, ginger, ground coriander, fresh coriander and sesame oil and blend together to a coarse paste. Add this laksa paste to the heated pan and stir-fry for 1 minute, then pour in the coconut milk and stock and bring to the boil. Simmer for 10 minutes to allow the flavours to combine and until slightly reduced, stirring occasionally.

3 Place the noodles in a large pan of boiling salted water and immediately remove from the heat. Set aside for 3–4 minutes, depending on the manufacturer's instructions, then drain and refresh under cold running water. Set aside. Blanch the sugar snap peas in a small pan of boiling salted water, drain and refresh under cold running water. Set aside.

4 Add the fish sauce to the coconut-milk mixture with the monkfish and stir gently for just a few seconds. Add the chargrilled squid and the prawns and stir gently for another few seconds until the prawns are just cooked and opaque in colour. Divide the cooked noodles between serving bowls and scatter the sugar snap peas on top. Ladle over the coconut broth and sprinkle the mint and basil leaves and the spring onions on top to serve.

53 Shellfish Risotto

SERVES 4

1 kg/2¹/₄ lb mussels, cleaned

200 ml/7 fl oz dry white wine

600 ml/1 pint fresh fish stock (from a carton is fine)

3 tbsp extra-virgin olive oil

75 g/3 oz unsalted butter, chilled and diced

1 onion, finely chopped

2 garlic cloves, finely chopped

2.5-cm/1-in piece fresh root ginger, peeled and finely grated

1 red chilli, seeded and finely chopped

350 g/12 oz arborio (risotto) rice

pinch saffron strands, soaked in a little warm water

225 g/8 oz squid, cleaned and sliced

225 g/8 oz raw tiger or Dublin Bay prawns, peeled and veins removed

2 plum tomatoes, peeled, seeded and diced

2 tbsp torn fresh basil

2 tbsp chopped fresh flatleaf parsley

salt and freshly ground black pepper

One of Italy's great simple dishes, perfect comfort food and still very fashionable at the moment. To me risottos are normally great standby supper or lunch dishes, but this one is just that bit more special. It's a wonderful summer dish and one that always sells well in the restaurant. The trick of a good risotto is to add the stock little by little, allowing the liquid to be almost completely absorbed before adding the next ladleful.

1 Place the mussels in a pan with 50 ml/2 fl oz of the wine. Cover tightly and cook over a high heat for a few minutes, shaking the pan occasionally, until all the mussels have opened – discard any that do not. Strain through a sieve, reserving the cooking liquor. Remove the meat from mussels and reserve. Place the stock in a pan and strain in the cooking liquor, leaving behind any grit. Bring to a gentle simmer.

2 Heat 2 tablespoons of the oil and 25 g/1 oz of the butter in a sauté pan. Add the onion, garlic, ginger and chilli and cook for about 5 minutes until softened but not browned, stirring occasionally. Stir in the rice and cook for a few minutes until nutty and perfumed. Add the remaining wine and allow to bubble away, stirring. Add a ladleful of the simmering stock and cook gently, stirring, until absorbed. Continue to add stock in this way, adding the saffron mixture after about 10 minutes – the whole process takes 20–25 minutes – until the rice is tender but still al dente.

3 Heat the remaining oil in a wok. Add the squid and prawns and stir-fry for 1-2 minutes, then add the tomatoes, basil, parsley and reserved mussel meat, toss together and remove from the heat. About 2 minutes before the arborio rice is cooked, fold in the shellfish mixture and then fold in the remaining butter, stirring until emulsified. Ladle into wide-rimmed bowls and serve at once.

54 Smoked Haddock and Salmon Pie with Tiger Prawns

No. 5   CLASSIC DISHES

SERVES 6–8

1 kg/2¼ lb floury potatoes, such as Maris Piper, cut into chunks

100 g/4 oz unsalted butter

450 ml/¾ pint milk

150 ml/¼ pint double cream

2 fresh bay leaves

1 whole clove

pinch freshly grated nutmeg

225 g/8 oz salmon fillet (in one piece)

225 g/8 oz undyed smoked haddock fillet (in one piece)

1 onion, finely diced

50 g/2 oz plain flour

4 hard-boiled eggs (preferably free-range or organic)

1 tsp anchovy essence

2 tbsp chopped fresh flatleaf parsley

½ tsp fresh soft thyme leaves

1 tsp English mustard powder

225 g/8 oz raw tiger prawns, peeled and veins removed

50 g/2 oz Gruyère cheese, grated

25 g/1 oz freshly grated Parmesan cheese

salt and freshly ground black pepper

green salad, to serve

A real nursery dish that is forever satisfying, and easy to prepare ahead. My fish pie uses undyed smoked haddock as it gives such a wonderful flavour and I've also added some salmon. I like mine topped with potatoes: some people prefer pastry, but you can't beat buttery, cheesy mash. Serve it with a fresh green salad for simplicity.

1 Preheat the oven to 200°C/400°F/Gas 6; fan oven 180°C from cold. Place the potatoes in a pan of boiling salted water, cover and simmer for 15–20 minutes until completely tender. Drain and return to the pan for a couple of minutes to dry out, shaking the pan occasionally to prevent the potatoes sticking to the bottom. Mash the potatoes or pass through a potato ricer or vegetable mouli if you like a really smooth finish. Beat in half of the butter and season to taste.

2 Place the milk in a sauté pan with the cream, bay leaves, clove and nutmeg. Add the salmon and haddock fillets and poach for 6–8 minutes until the fish is just tender. Transfer the fish fillets to a plate with a fish slice and, when they are cool enough to handle, flake the flesh, discarding any skin and bones. Set aside. Strain the poaching liquid and set aside.

3 Melt the remaining butter in a large, non-stick pan. Add the onion and cook for 6–8 minutes until it has softened but not coloured, stirring occasionally. Add the flour and cook for 3 minutes, stirring continuously. Pour in the reserved poaching liquid, a little at a time, whisking continuously after each addition. Once all the liquid has been added, reduce the heat and simmer gently for 10 minutes, stirring occasionally until slightly reduced and thickened.

4 Shell the eggs, and chop. Stir into the white sauce with the anchovy essence, parsley, thyme and mustard powder. Fold in the reserved flaked fish and season to taste. Remove from the heat and leave to cool, then fold in the raw prawns.

5 Spoon the fish mixture into an ovenproof dish of at least 2.25 litres/4 pints capacity. Allow a light skin to form, then carefully spread over the mashed potatoes to cover. Smooth with a palette knife and fluff up with a fork. Mix together the Gruyère and Parmesan and sprinkle over the top, then bake for 30–35 minutes or until the pie is bubbling and golden. Serve at once with green salad.

55 Plaice Tempura and Chips with Tartare Sauce

No. 6   CLASSIC DISHES

SERVES 4

2 litres/3¹/₂ pints sunflower or vegetable oil

900 g/2 lb potatoes, such as Desirée or King Edward

4 x 250 g/9 oz plaice fillets

malt vinegar, for seasoning

FOR THE TEMPURA BATTER:

100 g/4 oz plain flour

100 g/4 oz cornflour

350 ml/12 fl oz iced sparkling water

FOR THE TARTARE SAUCE:

250 ml/8 fl oz mayonnaise (home-made or shop-bought)

2 tbsp baby gherkins (cornichons), chopped

2 tbsp chopped fresh tarragon

2 tbsp chopped fresh flatleaf parsley

1 shallot, chopped

1 tsp Dijon mustard

¹/₂ lemon, pips removed

salt and freshly ground black pepper

Fish and chips is as English as Blackpool or Scarborough, traditionally cooked in pork dripping (I know it sounds ghastly, but it's not). Not just a take-away, this dish can be made at home without too much effort. Fierce battles rage over how best to make the perfect fried fish, but I have to say this particular batter is lovely and crisp – soggy fish is horrid. Served Japanese-style and with the perfect chips, this is perfect for any day of the week.

1 Preheat the oven to 150°C/300°F/Gas 2; fan oven 130°C from cold. To make the tartare sauce, place the mayonnaise in a bowl and stir in the gherkins, tarragon, parsley, shallot and mustard. Squeeze in lemon juice to taste and season generously. Transfer to a serving bowl, stir to combine and cover with plastic film, then chill until ready to serve.

2 Peel the potatoes, cut them into chunky chips and place in a bowl of water – this helps to remove the starch. Pour all the sunflower or vegetable oil into a deep-sided pan, making sure it is only half-full, and heat to 160°C/325°F. Drain the chips and then dry as much as possible in a clean tea towel before placing them in a wire basket and lowering them into the heated oil. Cook for 4 minutes until cooked through but not coloured. Drain well on kitchen paper and set aside.

3 To make the tempura batter, mix together the flour and cornflour in a bowl and then whisk in the iced sparkling water. Do not worry about lumps, as these will improve the texture of the batter, which needs to be used straight away. Dip the plaice fillets into the batter and then quickly lower into the heated oil and cook for 6–8 minutes until crisp and golden brown. Drain on kitchen paper and keep warm in the oven – this should be only for a minute or two so the batter doesn't lose any of its crispness.

4 Increase the temperature of the oil to 190°C/375°F. Tip the blanched chips back into the wire basket and then carefully lower into the heated oil. Cook for a minute or two until crisp and golden brown. Drain well on kitchen paper and serve immediately with the fish on greaseproof paper, wrapped, if you like, in traditional newspaper. Season with salt and vinegar and serve with the bowl of tartare sauce to pass around.

56 Gigot de Mer

SERVES 4

1.5 kg/3 lb piece monkfish tail

2 roasted red peppers (from a jar or can), cut into quarters

3 tbsp shredded fresh basil

12 thin slices Parma ham, about 175 g/6 oz in total

2 tbsp extra-virgin olive oil

40 g/1¹/₂ oz unsalted butter

2 leeks, trimmed and thinly sliced, about 225 g/8 oz in total

350 g/12 oz potatoes, cubed

600 ml/1 pint fresh chicken stock (from a carton is fine)

350 g/12 oz frozen or fresh podded peas

5 tbsp double cream

¹/₂ lemon, pips removed

salt and freshly ground black pepper

So why Gigot de Mer? Well, the French call monkfish *gigot de mer* because they think that it looks like a leg of lamb!

1 Ask your fishmonger to skin the monkfish tail, cut out the backbone (leaving 5 cm/2 in attached to the flesh end of the tail) and trim away all the pink and grey membrane from outside the fillets. When you get home rinse it well and pat dry with kitchen paper. Alternatively you can always have a go at preparing the fish yourself – it really is not that difficult.

2 Preheat the oven to 190°C/375°F/Gas 5; fan oven 170°C from cold. Season the cavity of the monkfish from which the bone has been removed. Arrange the peppers and two-thirds of the basil along the cut face of each fillet and then bring the two halves together, sandwiching the pepper mixture. Lay the Parma ham slices out on a work surface, slightly overlapping and covering an area the length of the stuffed tail, then place the tail on top and wrap the Parma ham around the fish. If it's not keeping together properly, tie it with butcher's string at 2.5-cm/1-in intervals. Place in a roasting tin and drizzle with 1 tablespoon of the oil. Roast for 30–35 minutes until the fish feels firm to the touch and the Parma ham is crisp, turning once so that all the Parma ham goes crispy.

3 Heat 25 g/1 oz of the butter and the remaining oil in a heavy-based pan. Add the leeks, cover and cook gently for about 15 minutes until softened but not coloured, stirring occasionally. Add the potatoes and pour in the stock, then bring to the boil. Reduce the heat and simmer for 10 minutes. Add the peas, cover and simmer for 8 minutes until everything is tender. Strain, reserving the cooking liquid, then place the cooking liquid in a pan and reduce to 120 ml/4 fl oz. Place the vegetables in a food processor with the cream and blitz to make a purée. Season and keep warm.

4 Remove the monkfish from the oven and transfer to a carving plate, leaving to rest for a couple of minutes. Slice it across into 2.5-cm/1-in slices. Strain any juices into the reduced cooking liquid, squeeze in the lemon juice to taste and boil fast for 4 minutes. Remove from the heat and add the remaining basil and butter, whisking to combine. Season. Divide the pea purée between serving plates, arrange the monkfish on top and spoon around the sauce to serve.

57 Seared Swordfish with Salsa Fresca

SERVES 4

2 tbsp olive oil

2 garlic cloves, finely chopped

1 red chilli, seeded and finely chopped

$1/2$ tsp ground cumin

$1/2$ tsp ground coriander

juice of 2 limes

4 x 175–225 g/6–8 oz swordfish steaks

225 g/8 oz small cherry tomatoes, halved

1 ripe, firm avocado, peeled, stoned and chopped

1 small red onion, finely chopped

2 tbsp chopped fresh coriander

pinch sugar

salt and freshly ground black pepper

green salad, to serve

The best way to treat fish nowadays is simply. The freshest swordfish is marinated and then cooked over a very high heat to seal the outside and create a crisp exterior, while the inside of the fish remains moist, almost raw. This recipe is perfect for lazy summer days and could be cooked with very little effort on the barbecue. You might want to serve hunks of ciabatta bread to mop up all those delicious juices.

1 Place the oil in a shallow, non-metallic dish with half of the garlic, chilli, ground cumin and ground coriander. Add the juice of $1/2$ lime and season generously. Mix to combine, then add the swordfish steaks, turning to coat. Cover with plastic film and chill for at least 5 and up to 30 minutes to allow the flavours to develop.

2 To make the salsa, place the remaining garlic, chilli, ground cumin, ground coriander and lime juice in a bowl. Add the tomatoes, avocado, onion, fresh coriander and sugar. Season generously and mix gently to combine. Set aside.

3 Heat a griddle pan. Remove the swordfish steaks from the marinade, shaking off any excess. Add to the pan and chargrill for 2–3 minutes on each side or until well seared and just tender. Arrange on serving plates and spoon on the salsa. Serve at once with salad.

58 Salmon en Croûte with Dill Butter and Pea Watercress Purée

SERVES 4

450 g/1 lb salmon fillet, skinned and boned

75 g/3 oz unsalted butter

8 sheets filo pastry, thawed if frozen

salt and freshly ground black pepper

steamed new potatoes tossed in butter and chopped fresh dill, to serve

FOR THE DILL BUTTER:

175 g/6 oz unsalted butter, softened

1 tbsp chopped fresh dill

juice of $1/2$ lemon

FOR THE PEA AND WATERCRESS PURÉE:

50 g/2 oz unsalted butter

6 spring onions, thinly sliced

175 g/6 oz frozen or fresh podded peas

1 tsp caster sugar

300 ml/$1/2$ pint fresh vegetable stock (from a carton is fine)

100 g/4 oz watercress, well picked over

This is a classy 1960s or possibly 1970s dinner-party dish that I've brought right up to date with a twist. This Salmon en croûte not only looks and tastes fantastic but is also deceptively easy to make. Try to buy frozen authentic Greek filo pastry in your local supermarket.

1 To make the dill butter, place the butter in a bowl, add the dill and lemon juice and mix to combine. Season to taste, cover with plastic film and set aside.

2 To make the pea and watercress purée, heat a non-stick sauté pan. Melt half the butter until hot and foaming, then add the spring onions and cook for a few minutes until softened, stirring occasionally. Add the peas to the pan with the caster sugar, stock and remaining butter, stirring to combine. Cover with a circle of greaseproof paper and allow to sweat for 2–3 minutes. Remove the paper and add the watercress, then allow to cook for a further minute or until all the liquid has evaporated. Place in a food processor and blend until nearly smooth – you still want a little texture. Set aside until ready to use.

3 Cut the salmon fillet into two equal portions, then cut each portion in half again. Trim each one into an even-sized square and carefully cut in half horizontally. Season. Melt the butter in a small pan or in the microwave. Brush one sheet of the filo pastry with melted butter. Place another sheet on top and turn the two over. Brush what is now the top sheet with melted butter.

4 Place a spoonful of the pea purée in the middle of the filo and place the bottom half of a salmon fillet on top, spread over a little of the dill butter and cover with the top half of the salmon fillet. Gather the sides of the filo pastry together, trim down with a sharp knife and fold over to enclose completely, forming a purse shape. Repeat this process with the remaining salmon fillets, filo pastry and most of the melted butter. Lightly brush the salmon filo parcels with the remaining melted butter and arrange on a baking sheet. Cover loosely with plastic film and chill for at least 30 minutes to firm up – overnight is fine.

5 Pre-heat the oven to 200°C/400°F/Gas 6; fan oven 180°C from cold. Bake the salmon filo parcels for 10–12 minutes or until the pastry is lightly golden. Heat the remaining pea and watercress purée in a small pan and arrange small mounds on serving plates with the salmon filo parcels. Add the new potatoes to serve.

59 Scented salmon on roasted vegetables

SERVES 4

3 small carrots, halved

6 tbsp olive oil

2 garlic cloves, crushed

1 red chilli, seeded and finely chopped

1 tsp fresh thyme leaves

3 small parsnips, halved

12 large shallots, peeled and trimmed

1 small butternut squash, peeled, seeded and cut into quarters

50 g/2 oz unsalted butter

8 fresh bay leaves

3 tbsp chopped fresh chervil

2 long strips pared lime rind

1 tsp coarsely ground black pepper

4 x 175 g/6 oz salmon steaks

sea salt and freshly ground black pepper

Roasting is a great way to cook root vegetables as they're robust enough to cope with the intense heat, and it draws out the most wonderful flavours. Try using any root vegetable or combination you fancy. However, it's worth remembering that beetroot will stain all other root vegetables, so it's probably best to roast them on their own. Just make sure that all your vegetables are roughly the same size to ensure even cooking.

1 Preheat the oven to 190°C/375°F/Gas 5; fan oven 170°C from cold. Place the carrots in a pan of boiling water and blanch for 2–3 minutes, then refresh under cold running water to retain their colour. Place 4 tablespoons of the oil in a roasting tin and add the garlic, chilli and thyme. Add all of the vegetables, including the carrots, and toss well to combine. Season generously and bake for 40–45 minutes or until the vegetables are completely tender and lightly caramelized, tossing from time to time to ensure they cook evenly.

2 About 5 minutes before the vegetables are ready, heat the remaining oil and the butter in a large frying pan. Add the bay leaves, chervil, lime rind and pepper and cook for 2 minutes, stirring. Add the salmon and cook for 2–3 minutes on each side for medium-rare or 1–2 minutes longer if you prefer your salmon well done. Arrange the roasted vegetables on serving plates and top with the salmon steaks, then spoon over the pan juices to serve.

60 Pumpkin Risotto with Leek and Mascarpone

SERVES 6–8

75 g/3 oz unsalted butter

350 g/12 oz pumpkin, peeled, seeded and diced

2 leeks, sliced

1 tbsp chopped fresh sage

about 2 litres/3^{1}/$_2$ pints fresh vegetable stock (from a carton is fine)

2 onions, finely chopped

1 heaped tsp fresh thyme leaves

1 fresh bay leaf

450 g/1 lb arborio (risotto) rice

300 ml/^{1}/$_2$ pint dry white wine

75 g/3 oz freshly grated Parmesan cheese

175 g/6 oz mascarpone cheese

4 tbsp chopped fresh flatleaf parsley

salt and freshly ground black pepper

dressed bitter salad leaves, to serve

Use leftovers from this dish to make risotto cakes – crunchy on the outside and rich and creamy in the middle. Simply roll and flatten handfuls of cold risotto into patties. Coat in a mixture of bread-crumbs and freshly grated Parmesan cheese before frying in butter until golden. To make your own stock, onions and carrots are pretty much essential, and tomatoes add welcome flavour, but beyond that use whatever vegetables you fancy. Just throw a few handfuls into a stockpot, cover with water, bring to the boil, put a lid on and simmer for 4 hours. Pass through a sieve and use as required.

1 Melt half of the butter in a large sauté pan, add the pumpkin and cook over a fairly high heat for about 5 minutes until lightly caramelized, tossing occasionally. Reduce the heat, add the leeks and sage, and cook over a gentle heat for another 2–3 minutes, stirring occasionally, until softened but not coloured and the pumpkin is completely tender when pierced with the tip of a sharp knife. Season, tip into a bowl and set aside until ready to use.

2 Pour the stock into a large pan and bring to a gentle simmer. Wipe out the pan in which the pumpkin mixture was cooked and return to the heat. Add the remaining butter, then tip in the onions, thyme and bay leaf and cook for a few minutes until softened but not coloured, stirring.

3 Add the rice to the onion mixture and continue to cook for another minute, stirring to ensure that all the grains are well coated. Pour in the wine and allow to reduce down, stirring until it is completely absorbed.

4 Begin to add the simmering stock a ladleful at a time, stirring frequently. Allow each stock addition to be almost completely absorbed before adding the next ladleful. After approximately 20 minutes, add the pumpkin mixture, the Parmesan, mascarpone and parsley, and stir energetically to combine. Season to taste and serve immediately with a big bowl of salad leaves.

61 Perfect Pizza Dough

250–350 ml/8–12 fl oz lukewarm water (45°C/113°F)

1 tbsp active dried yeast (7 g sachet)

550 g/1$^1/_4$ lb strong white flour, plus extra for dusting

1 tsp salt

$^1/_2$ tsp ground black pepper

2 tsp clear honey

2 tbsp extra-virgin olive oil, plus extra for brushing

If you don't want to use the dough at once or all in one go, punch it down and divide into portions as described in step 4, then place each one in a floured polythene bag. The dough should keep in the fridge for 2–3 days without any problems. When you want to use the dough, remove it from the fridge 2 hours before you need it – the room temperature re-awakens the yeast and off you go!

1 Pour 150 ml/$^1/_4$ pint of the lukewarm water into a bowl and sprinkle over the yeast. Stir to dissolve, then leave to rest in a warm place for 10 minutes. Sift the flour, salt and pepper into a large bowl. Stir the honey and olive oil into the yeast mixture until well combined.

2 Make a well in the centre of the dry ingredients and pour in the yeast mixture, mixing with your hands or a wooden spoon to form a soft and slightly sticky dough, and adding enough of the remaining water, little by little, until you have achieved the correct consistency.

3 Transfer the dough to a lightly floured work surface and then lightly flour your hands. Knead for 10 minutes until the dough is smooth and pliable. Lightly oil a bowl, which should be large enough for the dough to double in bulk. Place the dough in the bowl and lightly oil the top. Cover with cling film and set aside in a warm place for 1–2 hours until the dough has doubled in size.

4 When the dough has doubled in size, remove the cling film and, with a clenched fist, punch it down. Remove from the bowl and knead for a couple of minutes until smooth. Using a knife, cut the dough into 6 x 150 g/5 oz pieces and shape each piece into a smooth, round ball. Place on an oiled baking sheet and lightly oil the top of each ball, then cover with plastic film. If you are not going to use them straight away, place in the fridge as described above. Otherwise, leave to rest for 10 minutes before shaping.

5 To shape the pizza dough, lift a ball of dough on to a lightly floured work surface and lightly flour the top. To form the outer rim, lightly flour your fingers and press the tips into the dough 1 cm/$^1/_2$ in from the edge. Repeat all around the pizza, making sure you do not touch and damage the outer rim. Inside the rim flatten the pizza dough with the tips of your fingers. Turn the dough over and repeat the process, again making the outer rim and dimpling down the centre of the pizza.

6 To stretch the pizza, lightly flour the work surface and your hands again. Pick up the dough and slap it hard on to the work surface. Repeat this action once or twice, then drape the dough over your clenched fists with the thumbs resting side by side, just inside the rim of the pizza. Apply a little pressure with both thumbs and continue to stretch out the dough from just inside the rim until it is a 20-cm/8-in circle – stretching from the centre would weaken the dough and could cause holes to form during cooking. Place the dough on a well-floured baking sheet (a square of parchment paper also works at a push – just be careful of burning your hands and wear oven gloves).

62 Potato and Rocket Pizza

MAKES 2X20-CM/8-IN PIZZAS

550 g/1¹/₄ lb potatoes

4 tbsp extra-virgin olive oil

2 garlic cloves, crushed

2 x 150 g/5 oz Perfect Pizza Dough (p. 98), stretched

dried chilli flakes

2 heaped tbsp freshly grated Parmesan cheese

salt

good handful rocket leaves, stems removed and cut into strips

My pizza hero is Wolfgang Puck, owner of several restaurants in California, who made his name with the designer pizza. This is a variation on one of them, showing that a good pizza doesn't necessarily have to have tomatoes on it. If you don't have a pizza stone or tile, cook the pizza on a well-floured baking sheet.

1 Preheat the oven to 180°C/350°F/Gas 4; fan oven 160°C from cold. Peel the potatoes and cut into 5-mm/¹/₄-in slices: you can do this by hand or with a mandolin. Rinse well and pat dry with kitchen paper, then place in a bowl and toss in 2 tablespoons of the oil until lightly coated. Arrange on baking sheets in a single layer and roast for 20–25 minutes until they are just cooked through and beginning to turn golden, tossing once or twice. Transfer to a plate to cool a little and sprinkle with salt to taste.

2 Place the pizza stone or tile, if you have one, on the bottom of the oven and increase the heat of the oven to maximum for 1 hour. Place the remaining oil in a small bowl and stir in the garlic until well combined. Brush half over both pizza doughs and sprinkle over chilli flakes to taste. Arrange the potatoes on top in an overlapping layer. Brush with the remaining oil mixture and scatter over the Parmesan. Place in the oven, one at a time, for 8– 10 minutes or until the rims are golden brown. Remove from the oven and scatter over the rocket. Serve at once.

63 Caramelized Onion, Gorgonzola and Rosemary Pizza

MAKES 2X20-CM/8-IN PIZZAS

1 tbsp extra-virgin olive oil

25 g/1 oz unsalted butter

3 Spanish onions, halved and thinly sliced

2 x 150 g/5 oz *Perfect Pizza Dough* (p. 98), stretched

$^1/_4$ tsp finely chopped fresh rosemary

100–175 g/4–6 oz Gorgonzola cheese, crumbled

salt and freshly ground black pepper

A thin pizza base is a wonderful vehicle for all sorts of toppings and the onions, Gorgonzola and rosemary on this pizza are a scrumptiously pungent combination. You really need a wood-burning pizza oven to produce the high temperatures and the delicious smoky flavour. There is now a selection available for the garden from good garden centres or by mail order (check the classified section of food magazines or the Sunday broadsheets). If you don't have a pizza stone or tile, use a well-floured baking sheet.

1 Place a pizza stone or tile, if you have one, on the bottom of the oven and heat to maximum for 1 hour. Heat the oil and butter in a large sauté or frying pan. Add the onions and start by cooking over a fairly high heat, stirring constantly, until they begin to soften but not brown, then reduce the heat and continue to cook over a medium heat until caramelized, stirring frequently so the onions do not stick. This can take anything from about 30 minutes to 1 hour in total. Remove from the heat and season generously. Leave to cool a little.

2 Spread the pizza doughs with the caramelized onions and scatter over the rosemary, then dot with the Gorgonzola. Place the pizzas in the oven, one at a time, for 8–10 minutes or until the rims are golden brown. Remove from the oven and add a sprinkling of pepper to serve.

64 Aubergine and Pesto Pizza

MAKES 2X20-CM/8-IN PIZZAS

25 g/1 oz fresh basil leaves

1 small garlic clove, peeled

25 g/1 oz freshly grated
Parmesan cheese

1 tbsp toasted pine nuts

extra-virgin olive oil

2 small aubergines, cut into
5-mm/¹/₄-in slices

2 x 150 g/5 oz *Perfect Pizza
Dough* (p. 98), stretched

salt and freshly ground black
pepper

This pizza is the perfect munching food for an evening in: log fire, good movie, what more could you ask for? If you haven't got a wood-burning oven, but do have a barbeque this is the next best thing: cook the pizza base on one side on the barbie or chargrill, turn it over and cover with toppings, then finish the pizza in the oven or, better still, under a hot grill. You can also cook the pizza in the oven on a well-floured baking sheet.

1 Preheat a griddle pan. To make the pesto, place the basil, garlic, Parmesan and pine nuts in a food processor or mini-blender and blend until finely chopped, then pour in enough oil to make a smooth purée – you'll probably need about 5 tablespoons in total. Season to taste.

2 Brush each of the aubergine slices with a little oil and chargrill in batches for 4–5 minutes, turning once, until just tender. Place in a non-metallic dish and leave to cool a little, then add 4 tablespoons of the pesto. Turn to coat, cover with cling film and leave to marinate for 1–2 hours (overnight is best) in the fridge.

3 Place a pizza stone or tile, if you have one, on the bottom of the oven and heat to maximum for 1 hour. Spread the pizza doughs with some of the remaining pesto and arrange the aubergines on top in an overlapping layer. Place the pizzas in the oven, one at a time, for 8–10 minutes or until the rims are golden brown. Remove from the oven and brush with any remaining pesto. Serve at once.

65 Shallot Tarte Tatin

SERVES 2–4

50 g/2 oz unsalted butter

550 g/1¼ lb shallots, soaked in boiling water for 5 minutes, drained, peeled and trimmed

300 ml/½ pint fresh vegetable stock (from a carton is fine)

200 g/7 oz sheet ready-rolled puff pastry (from a 425 g/ 15 oz packet), thawed

2 tbsp caster sugar

1 tbsp balsamic vinegar

salt and freshly ground black pepper

leaf salad, to serve

The Belgian Chicory Board asked me to create a chicory recipe – I created a chicory tarte tatin – but it also works well with shallots. The sweet combination of the sugar and shallots is delicious. It is completely addictive: eat a wedge and you'll want more. The leftover stock from poaching the shallots makes an excellent base for a sauce or in a soup. Be careful when you invert the cooked tart on to a plate: hot butter and sugar can cause a nasty burn.

1 Heat a large frying or sauté pan. Melt 40 g/1½ oz of the butter in the pan, add the shallots and gently fry for about 10 minutes until golden, tossing occasionally. Pour in the stock and simmer for another 5–10 minutes, depending on the size of the shallots, until they are tender when pierced with a sharp knife but still holding their shape. Remove the shallots with a slotted spoon, drain well and pat dry with kitchen paper. Leave to cool completely.

2 Preheat the oven to 190°C/375°F/Gas 5; fan oven 170°C from cold. Unroll the pastry and cut out a 25-cm/10-in circle, using a large plate as a template (don't worry if the edges of the pastry sheet fall a bit short). Transfer to a floured baking sheet and chill for at least 30 minutes to allow the pastry to rest.

3 Melt the remaining knob of butter in a 23-cm/9-in oven-proof frying pan (preferably non-stick). Add the shallots and toss until well coated and heated through. Sprinkle over the sugar and cook for a minute or two until caramelized, tossing constantly. Sprinkle over the vinegar, toss again until well coated and remove from the heat.

4 Season the shallots generously. Place the disc of pastry on top of the shallots, tucking the edges down the side of the pan. Bake for about 30 minutes or until the pastry is well risen and golden brown. Leave for a few minutes before loosening the sides with a knife and inverting on to a flat plate. Serve warm or cold, cut into slices, with salad.

66 Aubergine Charlotte

SERVES 6–8

6 red peppers

2 large aubergines, cut into 5-mm/¼-in slices

olive oil, for cooking

350 g/12 oz small new salad potatoes, cut into 1-cm/½-in slices

225 g/8 oz spinach, thick stalks and ribs removed

2 x 250 g/9 oz cartons ricotta cheese

100 g/4 oz freshly grated Parmesan cheese

3 eggs (preferably free-range or organic)

4 heaped tbsp snipped fresh chives

salt and freshly ground black pepper

green salad, to serve

FOR THE ROCKET SALSA:

50 g/2 oz rocket leaves

25 g/1 oz fresh flatleaf parsley leaves

2 large garlic cloves, roughly chopped

2 tbsp rinsed capers (preferably salted)

1 tbsp red wine vinegar

1 tbsp Dijon mustard

150 ml/¼ pint olive oil

This is a very impressive vegetarian main course. If you don't want to go to the bother of roasting your own peppers, you can always buy a couple of jars of roasted peppers, which would work just as well – but make sure you wipe off all the excess oil with kitchen paper or you'll run the risk of making the charlotte too greasy. For a change you could also substitute the first layer of peppers with sliced artichoke hearts that have been preserved in oil.

1 Preheat the grill and a griddle pan. Arrange the peppers on a grill rack and cook for 20–30 minutes turning occasionally, until well blackened and blistered, then place in a large polythene bag and secure. Set aside until completely cool, then remove the cores, cut into quarters and peel off the skin, discarding the seeds. Lightly brush each aubergine slice with a little oil and cook in batches on the griddle pan until tender and lightly charred. Drain on kitchen paper.

2 Place the potatoes in a pan of boiling salted water, cover and simmer for 8–10 minutes until just tender. Drain and leave to cool completely. Heat a little oil in a separate pan and quickly wilt the spinach. Season to taste, remove from the heat and leave to cool, then squeeze dry and chop. Place the ricotta in a large bowl with the Parmesan, eggs and chives. Add ½ teaspoon each salt and pepper and beat until well combined.

3 Preheat the oven to 200°C/400°F/Gas 6; fan oven 180°C from cold. Line a 23-cm/9-in oven-proof dish or cake tin that is 7.5 cm/3 in deep with non-stick baking paper. Arrange some of the aubergine slices in an overlapping layer on the bottom of the dish and then use some more slices to line right up the sides, making sure there are no gaps and reserving enough to cover the top.

4 Spread the spinach in an even layer over the aubergines and then add a third of the ricotta mixture. Add the potatoes in an overlapping layer and then cover with another layer of the ricotta mixture. Use half of the peppers to make a layer, then add the remaining ricotta mixture and finish with the remaining peppers, again ensuring that there are no gaps. Finally cover with the reserved aubergine slices and press down firmly to help cement the layers together.

contd. overleaf

5 Cover with a circle of non-stick baking paper and place the dish on a baking sheet. Bake for 1 hour or until the charlotte is completely heated through and the cheese layers have set. Remove from the oven, take off the baking-paper circle and leave to rest for about 5 minutes, soaking up any excess oil with kitchen paper.

6 To make the rocket salsa, coarsely chop the rocket, parsley, garlic and capers together or pulse in a food processor or mini-blender – you get a better result by hand.

7 Transfer the salsa to a clean jam jar with a lid and gradually stir in the vinegar, mustard and oil. Season to taste, remembering that the capers are already quite salty anyway. Shake well to combine.

8 To turn the charlotte out, place the baking sheet on top of the dish and quickly turn over, then lift off the dish and carefully remove the baking paper, again soaking up any excess oil with kitchen paper. Cut into slices with a carving knife and serve warm or cold with the rocket salsa and salad.

67 Onion and Goats' Cheese Frittata

SERVES 4

2 tbsp olive oil

25 g/1 oz unsalted butter

3 Spanish onions, thinly sliced

1 tsp fresh thyme leaves

3 garlic cloves, crushed

8 large eggs (preferably free-range or organic), beaten

25 g/1 oz freshly grated Parmesan cheese

1 tsp finely chopped fresh sage

100 g/4 oz mild, creamy goats' cheese, crumbled

salt and freshly ground black pepper

tomato salsa (good-quality, shop-bought is fine), to serve

This is one of my favourite frittatas, the sweetness of the onions complementing the creaminess of the goats' cheese perfectly. It is as good served cold as hot or warm. Originating from Sicily, it is cooked until set firm, making it excellent as picnic food or an addition to a platter of antipasti, as well as a fine light lunch or supper. And I know it's not good to pick, but I love going home and finding the leftovers of a frittata in the fridge – it's the perfect midnight snack.

1 Heat 1 tablespoon of the oil with the butter in a large sauté or frying pan. Add the onions and start by cooking over a medium heat, stirring constantly, until they begin to soften but not brown, then reduce the heat and continue to cook over a low heat, stirring frequently so the onions do not stick. They will need about 30 minutes in total to caramelize. Stir in the thyme and garlic 5 minutes before the end of the cooking time. Tip into a large bowl and leave to cool for at least 5 minutes. Season generously.

2 Preheat the oven to 180°C/350°F/Gas 4; fan oven 160°C from cold. Add the eggs, Parmesan and sage to the onions and stir well to combine – you should have 1.2 litres/2 pints of mixture in total. Heat the remaining oil in an ovenproof heavy-based pan of about 23 cm/9 in diameter and deep enough to take the mixture. Swirl to coat the sides of the pan evenly, then pour in the egg mixture and cook for 2 minutes over a low heat to set the bottom and sides. Scatter over the goats' cheese and cook gently for another 5 minutes.

3 Transfer the pan to the oven and cook, uncovered, for about 20 minutes until just set, puffed up and lightly golden. Loosen the sides of the frittata with a palette knife, turn out onto a large plate and cut into wedges. Serve warm or cold, with a good dollop of salsa.

68 Wild Mushroom Cassoulet

SERVES 4–6

5 tbsp extra-virgin olive oil

1 large aubergine, cut into 1-cm/^{1}/$_2$-in cubes, about 350 g/12 oz in total

1 onion, roughly chopped

4 garlic cloves, finely chopped

75 g/3 oz unsalted butter

350 g/12 oz mixed wild mushrooms, sliced

1 glass dry white wine, about 150 ml/^{1}/$_4$ pint

25 g/1 oz dried porcini or cep mushrooms

1 tsp dried rosemary

1 tsp dried thyme

2 dried bay leaves, broken into small pieces

400 g/14 oz can white cannellini beans, drained and rinsed

400 g/14 oz can chopped tomatoes

750 g/1^1/$_2$ lb plum tomatoes, about 8 in total

50 g/2 oz fresh white breadcrumbs (preferably from a rustic-style loaf)

sea salt and coarsely ground black pepper

Dijon Mash (p. 110), to serve

This is a great dish if you want to keep both meat-eaters and vegetarians happy. Simply serve the cassoulet with some good-quality sausages – try pork and leek or venison. I like to serve this with Dijon mash, but warm crusty bread and a bitter leaf salad also go very well.

1 Preheat the oven to 180°C/350°F/Gas 4; fan oven 160°C from cold. Heat a large sauté pan, add 4 tablespoons of the oil and fry the aubergine for 10–15 minutes, tossing occasionally, until completely tender and dark golden. Season to taste and transfer to a bowl with a slotted spoon. Add the remaining oil to the same pan and gently fry the onion and garlic for about 8 minutes until the onion has softened but not coloured, stirring occasionally. Remove from the pan with a slotted spoon and tip on top of the aubergine.

2 Melt 25 g/1 oz of the butter in the oil that is left in the pan. Add the wild mushrooms and stir-fry over a high heat for about 3–4 minutes until they have started to colour and release their juices, then add them to the aubergine mixture. Pour the wine into the pan and allow it to bubble down, stirring to remove any sediment from the bottom, then pour into the aubergine mixture.

3 Meanwhile, place the dried porcini or ceps in a spice or coffee grinder, or a mini-blender, and add the rosemary, thyme, bay leaves and ^{1}/$_2$ teaspoon of coarsely ground black pepper. Blend to a fine powder – you may have to do this in batches, depending on the size of your machine. Add to the aubergine mixture, then add the beans and canned tomatoes, stirring to combine. Tip the mixture into a large, ovenproof dish that will hold at least 1.75 litres/3 pints. Blanch the plum tomatoes in boiling water for 30 seconds and remove the skins, then cut in half, cut away the cores and scoop out the seeds. Arrange the tomato halves, uncut-side up, on top of the vegetable mixture and season to taste.

4 Melt the remaining butter in a small pan or in the microwave and stir in the breadcrumbs. Season to taste. Scatter on top of the tomatoes, making sure the breadcrumbs get into all of the crevices, but don't cover the tomatoes completely, then bake for about 35–40 minutes until bubbling and the breadcrumbs are golden brown. Serve at once with the *Dijon Mash*.

69 Roast Walnut Pesto with Spaghetti

SERVES 4–6

50 g/2 oz walnuts (preferably freshly shelled)

4 large spinach leaves, ribs removed

1 tbsp fresh flatleaf parsley leaves

25 g/1 oz fresh basil leaves

3 garlic cloves, roughly chopped

50 g/2 oz freshly grated Parmesan or Pecorino Sardo cheese, plus extra for garnishing

150 ml/¹/₄ pint extra-virgin olive oil, plus a little extra (optional)

2 tbsp ricotta cheese (optional)

450 g/1 lb dried spaghetti

sea salt and freshly ground black pepper

This makes a nice change from your average basil pesto. Ricotta is not a traditional ingredient in pesto, but it does help to keep the sauce emulsified. However, you'll have to use the pesto within a couple of days. This pesto is also delicious swirled into tomato soup, or try stuffing some underneath the skin of a chicken breast before cooking. I also like to use it as a dressing for salads or spread on to crostini and topped with bubbling goats' cheese – the possibilities are endless!

1 Preheat the oven to 180°C/350°F/Gas 4; fan oven 160°C from cold. Spread out the walnuts on a baking sheet and roast for 8–10 minutes until lightly toasted. Remove from the oven and leave to cool completely. Place the spinach and parsley in a small pan of boiling water and blanch for 30 seconds, then drain immediately and refresh under cold running water. Squeeze dry and place in a food processor with the basil, 1 teaspoon salt and the garlic, then blend until finely minced.

2 Add the walnuts and Parmesan or Pecorino Sardo to the food processor and blitz again briefly; then, with the machine running, pour in the oil through the feeder tube until the pesto is thickened and emulsified. Using a spatula, scrape the pesto mixture into a bowl and fold in the ricotta cheese, if you are going to use the pesto within a couple of days. Season to taste. You should have about 300 ml/¹/₂ pint in total. To preserve the pesto for longer, place the contents into a sterilized glass jar and coat the surface with a film of olive oil. Cover with a lid and chill. This will keep for up to 1 month: just ensure that you pour in a little extra olive oil after each time you use it.

3 To serve, bring a large pan of water to a rolling boil. Add a good pinch of salt, swirl in the spaghetti, stir once and cook for 8–12 minutes or according to the packet instructions until the pasta is al dente. Drain and tip back into the pan and pour in the pesto. Stir until all the spaghetti is well coated in the sauce, then divide among warmed wide-rimmed serving bowls. Sprinkle over some grated cheese and serve at once.

70 Ravioli with Marjoram and Mozzarella

SERVES 4–6

350 g/12 oz type '00' pasta flour, plus extra for dusting

2 eggs, plus 5 egg yolks

semolina flour, for dusting (fine, hard semolina)

200 g/7 oz ball mozzarella cheese (preferably buffalo), diced

100 g/4 oz freshly grated Parmesan cheese, plus extra shavings to garnish

100 g/4 oz ricotta cheese

1 tbsp chopped fresh marjoram, plus extra sprigs to garnish

pinch dried red chilli flakes

1 small garlic clove, finely chopped

300–600 ml/¹/₂–1 pint *Rich Tomato Sauce* **(p. 120)**

salt and freshly ground black pepper

The perfect method for cooking large quantities of ravioli is in a deep roasting tin placed directly on the heat. Simply pour in 5 cm/2 in water and place the tin directly over two burners. This helps the ravioli to cook much more evenly and without the damage, that sticking and stirring often cause.

1 Place the flour and ¹/₂ teaspoon salt in a food processor with the eggs and egg yolks and pulse until the mixture comes together in a loose ball. Tip out on to a lightly floured work surface, dust with semolina and knead for about 3 minutes until smooth. Cut into ten portions and knead into balls, then wrap in cling film and chill for at least 20 minutes (up to 2 hours is best).

2 Using a pasta machine, roll out each piece of dough, keeping the rest wrapped. Pass the dough through the widest setting three times, then narrow the setting as you roll out, until you have a thin, pliable pasta sheet, then pass through the thinnest setting three times. Repeat, covering the rolled-out sheets with a damp cloth.

3 To make the filling, place all the cheeses in a bowl. Stir in the marjoram, chilli flakes and garlic, then season to taste. Divide into twenty walnut-sized balls. Lay a sheet of the pasta on a lightly floured work surface and cut out four 10-cm/4-in squares. Place a ball of filling on two of the squares and, using a pastry brush, lightly brush the pasta with water around the filling; then cover with the remaining two squares. Gently pat the pasta down, making sure you extract all the air so that each ravioli is tightly sealed.

4 Take each ravioli and pull out the edges with your thumbs to thin them down, then trim with a ravioli cutter. Dust liberally in semolina flour. Repeat with the remaining sheets of pasta. They can now be cooked straight away or arranged on a tray dusted with semolina and kept covered with cling film for 3–4 hours in the fridge.

5 When you are ready to eat, place the tomato sauce in a small pan and bring to a gentle simmer just to heat through. Bring a large pan of salted water to the boil. Add the ravioli and cook gently for 3–4 minutes or until just tender. Drain carefully with a slotted spoon and arrange on serving plates. Drizzle around some of the tomato sauce and garnish with Parmesan shavings, marjoram sprigs and a sprinkling of black pepper to serve.

71 Yorkshire Puddings

SERVES 6–8

100 g/4 oz plain flour

4 eggs (preferably free-range or organic), beaten

200 ml/7 fl oz milk

4 tbsp beef dripping or sunflower oil

salt and freshly ground black pepper

If you've had problems with your Yorkshire puddings in the past, try my mate Brian Turner's recipe which he showed me on the BBC Television programme *Ready Steady Cook*. Serve them with *Roast Rib of Beef on the Bone* (p. 34).

1 Sift the flour and a pinch of salt into a bowl. Make a well in the centre, then pour in the beaten eggs and gradually draw in the flour. Add the milk and whisk until you have achieved a smooth batter, the consistency of single cream. Season to taste, cover with cling film and leave to rest for 1 hour, if time allows.

2 Preheat the oven to 220°C/425°F/Gas 7; fan oven 200°C from cold. Place the dripping or oil into 2 x twelve-hole bun-tin trays and heat on the top shelves of the oven for 5 minutes. The fat needs to be very hot to enable the puddings to rise quickly and to stop them sticking to the moulds. Stir the batter and then, using a small ladle, pour it into the hot fat so that it comes halfway up the sides. Bake the puddings for about 20 minutes until well risen, crisp and golden brown. Serve at once.

72 Dijon Mash

SERVES 4–6

1.5 kg/3 lb floury potatoes, peeled and cut into 2.5-cm/ 1-in cubes

about 120 ml/4 fl oz extra-virgin olive oil

1 bunch spring onions, finely chopped

2 tbsp Dijon mustard

salt and freshly ground black pepper

The French call their mashed potato 'pommes purées' and it is very different from our beloved mash. This mash should be so runny that it nearly pours! It can be prepared in advance and slowly reheated. I like to serve it with the Wild Mushroom Cassoulet (p. 106) or Boeuf Bourguignonne (p. 22). Floury potatoes make the best mash: choose from Golden Wonder, King Edward, Pentland Ivory and Pentland Hawk.

1 Place the potatoes in a large pan of boiling salted water. Bring to the boil, cover and simmer for 15–20 minutes until the potatoes are tender without breaking up. Drain and return to the pan over a low heat to dry out. Mash the potatoes, or pass them through a potato ricer or vegetable mouli if you want a really smooth finish.

2 Meanwhile, place the oil in a small pan with the spring onions and cook over a low heat for about 10 minutes without colouring to allow the flavours to infuse. Place the potatoes in a food processor with the mustard and season to taste. Turn on the machine and quickly pour in the oil mixture through the feeder tube to make a purée, but be careful not to overwork. Serve at once.

73 Potato and Turnip Bake

SERVES 6–8

40 g/1¹/₂ oz unsalted butter

450 g/1 lb potatoes, cut into wafer-thin slices (with a mandolin or by hand)

450 g/1 lb turnips, thinly sliced

1 garlic clove, finely chopped

1 tbsp fresh thyme leaves

600 ml/1 pint double cream

1 fresh bay leaf

salt and freshly ground black pepper

A variation on *gratin dauphinoise*, a favourite of mine, this is a rich, moreish dish that could be eaten on its own with just a fresh green salad, or served with roast or grilled meats. I find it is the perfect accompaniment for *Rack of Lamb with a Pistachio Crust* (p. 48).

1 Preheat the oven to 200°C/400°F/Gas 6; fan oven 180°C from cold. Rub a 1.5-litre/2¹/₂-pint ovenproof dish with a little of the butter. Place three-quarters of the potatoes and turnips in a large bowl, setting aside the remainder to use for decorating the top of the bake. Add the garlic, thyme and plenty of seasoning and lightly mix to combine.

2 Place the cream and bay leaf in a small pan and just heat through but do not allow the mixture to boil. Tip the flavoured potato and turnip slices into the oven-proof dish and decorate the top with the reserved slices in an overlapping layer. Pour the hot cream on top, discarding the bay leaf, and dot with the remaining butter. Bake for 45–50 minutes until the potatoes and turnips are completely tender. Serve at once.

74 Artichoke Rösti

SERVES 4-6

3 globe artichokes

juice of 2 lemons

450 g/1 lb waxy potatoes, such as Desirée

75 g/3 oz unsalted butter

4 tbsp snipped fresh chives

salt and freshly ground black pepper

Globe artichokes are loved by the Italians and the French – why not by the British? The trouble is that their preparation can be off-putting, but once you know what to do, you'll repeat the experience on a regular basis. Alternatively, use good-quality artichoke hearts preserved in olive oil: you'll need about ten for this recipe. Serve with poached eggs and hollandaise sauce or with *Calf's Liver and Pancetta with Balsamic Vinegar* (p. 32).

1 Place the artichokes in a pan of boiling salted water and add the lemon juice. Bring to the boil, reduce the heat and simmer for 15–30 minutes, depending on size, until the artichokes are completely tender. Drain well and leave to cool.

2 When the artichokes are cool enough to handle, peel away the outer leaves. Scrape away the choke, a tuft of whitish fibres, by scooping it off the flesh with a teaspoon or just by pulling it off with your fingers. You are left with the heart. Cut away the stalk using a sharp knife, then thinly shred the remainder.

3 Peel the potatoes and place in a pan of boiling salted water. Bring to the boil, reduce the heat and simmer for 12 minutes. Drain immediately and leave to cool.

4 When the potatoes are cool enough to handle, grate them into a large bowl using the coarse side of a grater. Melt 25 g/ 1 oz of the butter in a small pan or in the microwave, then stir into the potatoes with the chives and shredded artichoke hearts. Season generously, mix to combine and shape into eight 7.5-cm/3-in flat rounds.

5 Melt the remaining butter in a large, non-stick frying pan. Add the röstis and cook for 8–10 minutes, turning once, until cooked through and golden brown. Drain on kitchen paper and serve hot.

75 Jewelled Couscous

SERVES 6–8

600 ml/1 pint fresh chicken or vegetable stock (from a carton is fine)

500 g/1 lb 2 oz couscous

grated rind of 1 lemon

6 tbsp extra-virgin olive oil

50 g/2 oz toasted flaked almonds

100 g/4 oz ready-to-eat dried apricots, chopped

50 g/2 oz sultanas

2 heaped tbsp chopped fresh flatleaf parsley

2 heaped tbsp chopped fresh coriander

salt and freshly ground black pepper

Couscous can often be very dull and bland. So what I've done is make it into *Jewelled Couscous*, which is just lovely served with *Moroccan Lamb Tagine* (p. 42) or *Butterflied Leg of Lamb with Moroccan Mint Mechoui* (p. 41). It can be made a day in advance, left to cool completely and then covered with cling film and chilled until needed. To reheat, simply follow the instructions in step 3.

1 Heat the stock in a pan until boiling. Pour in the couscous in a thin, steady stream and then stir in the lemon rind. Cover with cling film and set aside for 5 minutes to allow the grains to swell. Remove the cling film and fluff up the grains with a fork so that they separate.

2 Return the couscous to the heat and drizzle over the olive oil. Cook gently for a few minutes, stirring with the fork to fluff up the grains, then remove from the heat. (You could also do this in a large steamer, lined with a piece of muslin or a couple of new J-cloths.) Fold in the almonds, apricots, sultanas, parsley and coriander and season to taste.

3 Tip the couscous into an ovenproof dish: you can keep it warm in the bottom of a moderate oven, covered with foil, for up to 30 minutes until ready to serve. Alternatively, allow to cool, cover with cling film or a tight-fitting lid, and chill until needed. To reheat in a microwave, pierce the cling film all over with a fork and heat on high for 2–3 minutes before serving.

76 Greens with Oyster Sauce

SERVES 4

450 g/1 lb mixed greens, chopped

2 tsp sesame oil

2 tsp groundnut or vegetable oil

2.5-cm/1-in piece fresh root ginger, peeled and finely grated

2 red chillies, seeded and finely chopped

2 garlic cloves, finely chopped

50 ml/2 fl oz oyster sauce

50 ml/2 fl oz Chinese rice wine (*mirin*) or dry sherry

50 ml/2 fl oz light soy sauce

1 tbsp clear honey

This is a very simple dish and one of my favourite ways of preparing Oriental greens. The blanching preserves the sweetness while the hot sauce gives the vegetables a rich, almost nutty flavour. It is excellent as an accompaniment for *Tea-smoked Barbary duck* (p. 75) as it provides a much-needed sauce. Use any selection of greens available, such as rocket, beet, turnip or mustard greens, Swiss chard, spinach or any of the Oriental greens which are now readily available in most supermarkets.

1 Bring a large pan of salted water to a rolling boil, add the greens and blanch for 1–3 minutes, depending on the combination of vegetables you are using, until wilted and tender. Drain well and place in a warmed serving dish. Keep warm.

2 Meanwhile, heat the sesame and the groundnut or vegetable oil in a small frying pan. Add the ginger, chillies and garlic and cook for 2 minutes, stirring, then blend in the oyster sauce, rice wine or sherry, soy sauce and honey. Just heat through and dribble over the greens to serve.

77 Saffron Pea Pilaff

SERVES 4–6

225 g/8 oz basmati rice

50 g/2 oz unsalted butter

25 g/1 oz flaked almonds

8 walnut halves, roughly chopped

25 g/1 oz raisins

8 ready-to-eat dried apricots, diced

4 whole cloves

2 cardamom pods

2.5-cm/1-in piece cinnamon stick

$1/2$ tsp saffron strands, soaked in a little warm water

4 spring onions, thinly sliced

600 ml/1 pint vegetable or chicken stock (made from 1 stock cube is fine)

375 g/13 oz frozen or fresh podded peas

3 tbsp chopped fresh coriander

salt and freshly ground black pepper

The combination of rice and peas seems to be popular worldwide, especially in the Caribbean, and this one from Kashmir is no exception. It has a great colour with a lovely blend of spices, nuts and fruit. Serve on its own or with *Butterflied Poussin* (p. 79). It is also a very worthy partner to any stew or tagine.

1 Rinse the rice under cold running water, then set aside to drain. Heat half of the butter in a large, heavy-based pan with a tight-fitting lid. Add the almonds, walnuts, raisins and apricots and cook for about 5 minutes until the nuts are golden brown and the raisins are plumped up, stirring occasionally and being careful that nothing burns. Tip out on to a plate and set aside.

2 Add the remaining butter to the same pan and then tip in the cloves, cardamom pods and cinnamon stick. Cook gently for a minute or two until they become aromatic, stirring continuously.

3 Add the drained rice to the pan and cook for 2 minutes, stirring to ensure that all the rice grains are coated in butter, then stir in the saffron mixture, the spring onions and $1/2$ teaspoon each salt and pepper. Pour in the stock, bring to the boil, then reduce the heat, cover and simmer for 20 minutes or until the rice is fluffed up and completely tender.

4 Just as the pilaff has nearly finished cooking, place the peas in a pan of boiling salted water and simmer for 2–3 minutes until tender. Drain. Remove the pilaff from the heat and add the freshly cooked peas, the coriander and reserved nut mixture. Gently fold in using a large metal spoon until well combined. Season to taste and serve hot.

78 Perfect Roast Potatoes

SERVES 4–6

1.5 kg/3 lb floury potatoes (preferably all similar in size)

dripping, goose fat or duck fat, for basting

about 2 heaped tbsp plain flour

1/2 tsp fresh thyme leaves (optional)

few whole unpeeled garlic cloves (optional)

salt and freshly ground black pepper

I am looking for really crunchy outsides and fluffy middles. Sounds obvious, doesn't it, but I'm amazed how often, when dining out, one is presented with roast potatoes that have been started off in the deep-fat fryer and finished in the oven. The method described below is the best I have found for guaranteed results. As regards what to cook them in, all fats freeze very well, so do make the effort if you have some left over from a roast – it really does make a world of difference to the flavour of your roast potatoes. Serve them with *Roast Rib of Beef on the Bone* (p. 34), *Roast Loin of Pork with Apple Sauce* (p. 60), *Salt-crusted Roast Chicken* (p. 78) or *Roast Turkey with Spiced Rub* (pp. 73–4).

1 Preheat the oven to 200°C/400°F/Gas 6; fan oven 180°C from cold. Peel the potatoes and cut into large, even-sized pieces. Place in a pan of cold salted water and bring to the boil. Simmer for 10 minutes, then drain and return to the pan for a minute or so to dry out.

2 Preheat a large roasting tin with a 1-cm/1/2-in depth of dripping, goose fat or duck fat for a few minutes until just smoking. Place the flour in a small bowl, season generously and add the thyme leaves (if using). Place the potatoes in a colander and toss them in a handful of the seasoned flour. You'll need to do this quite vigorously so the edges start to break up slightly.

3 Arrange the potatoes, flat-side down, in the hot fat and baste the tops, adding the garlic cloves at this point for an extra dimension, if liked. Place in the oven and cook for 20 minutes before turning the potatoes over. Cook for a further 20 minutes, then pour off most of the fat. Cook for a final 20 minutes until crispy around the edges and golden brown.

79 Crispy Potato Skins

SERVES 4–6

6 unpeeled potatoes, each about 100 g/4 oz

3 tbsp olive oil

1 tbsp finely chopped fresh rosemary

salt and freshly ground black pepper

These are always a winner and very cheap to make. Prepare up to 24 hours in advance, arrange in a roasting tin and cover with cling film. Chill until needed and cook immediately before serving. They are also suitable for deep-frying and literally take a matter of minutes. Serve with *Fingerlicking Ribs* (p. 54) or just on their own with a soured cream and chive dip.

1 Preheat the oven to 200°C/400°F/Gas 6; fan oven 180°C from cold. Prick each potato all over and rub with a little of the oil. Place them directly on the oven shelf and bake for 40–45 minutes until they feel slightly soft when squeezed, then leave to cool.

2 Cut each potato in half lengthways and then into quarters. Scoop out the flesh, retaining for another use such as mash, and leaving a layer of potato at least 5 mm/¼ in thick on the skin. Brush all over with the remaining oil and arrange in a single layer, skin-side down, on a wire rack set on a roasting tin. Season generously and sprinkle over the rosemary. Bake for 30 minutes, turning half way through, until crisp and golden brown. Serve hot.

80 Dumplings

SERVES 6–8

250 g/9 oz plain flour, plus extra for dusting

1 tsp salt

2 tsp baking powder

2 tbsp olive oil

4 tbsp chopped fresh flatleaf parsley

4 tbsp snipped fresh chives

150 ml/1/4 pint milk

These dumplings are best served with *Beef in Stout* (p. 36), but could also be served with all types of stew or hotpot, to make a refreshing change from mashed potato or rice as an accompanying dish.

1 Sift the flour, salt and baking powder into a large bowl. Make a well in the centre and add the oil and herbs (reserving a little of the parsley to garnish), then pour in the milk and, using a fork, mix to form a soft dough. Place the dough on a lightly floured surface and knead briefly. Shape the dough into sixteen walnut-sized dumplings. Cook and serve according to the recipe for *Beef in Stout*.

81 Horseradish Cream

MAKES ABOUT 200ml/7fl oz

5-cm/2-in piece fresh horseradish root

85 ml/3 fl oz double cream

50 ml/2 fl oz mayonnaise (home-made or from a jar)

1 tbsp Dijon mustard

1 1/2 tsp lemon juice

pinch sugar

salt and freshly ground black pepper

If you can't find fresh horseradish root, simply follow the recipe using 3 tablespoons of ready-grated horseradish, which you can buy in jars from most major supermarkets.

1 Peel and finely grate the horseradish root – and be prepared to cry! Place the cream in a bowl and whisk until lightly whipped.

2 Add the horseradish, mayonnaise, mustard, lemon juice and sugar to the cream. Season to taste and stir until well blended. Spoon into a serving bowl and chill until ready to serve.

82 Classic Parsley Sauce

SERVES 4

25 g/1 oz unsalted butter, plus a little extra

2 tbsp plain flour

300 ml/¹/₂ pint milk or reserved poaching milk (from the *Smoked Haddock Fish Cakes*, p. 83)

150 ml/¹/₄ pint double cream

3 tbsp chopped fresh flatleaf parsley

handful fresh sorrel leaves, shredded (optional)

salt and freshly ground white pepper

Parsley sauce does not seem to be in fashion at the moment, which is a real shame, because it is very useful, and, when made properly, delicious with the *Smoked Haddock Fish Cakes* (p. 83). For extra flavour use the reserved poaching milk from the fish cakes or infuse the milk by boiling it with an onion, clove and bay leaf for a minute or two. Sorrel has a wonderful citrus tang and adds an extra dimension to the sauce, but it can be difficult to get hold of. It is available in some of the major supermarkets, and you could always grow your own.

1 Melt the butter in a small pan. Add the flour and cook for 3 minutes, stirring over a low heat. Pour in the milk, a little at a time, beating vigorously after each addition, until smooth. Simmer gently for 10 minutes until smooth and thickened, stirring occasionally and adding more milk if necessary.

2 Add the cream to the sauce with the parsley and sorrel (if using) and reheat gently until the sorrel has just wilted. Season to taste. Dot the surface with a little butter to prevent a skin forming if you are not serving the sauce at once.

83 Rich Tomato Sauce

MAKES ABOUT 600 ML/1 PINT

4 tbsp extra-virgin olive oil

1 onion, finely diced

2 garlic cloves, finely diced

1 celery stick, finely diced

150 ml/¼ pint dry white wine

750 g/1½ lb plum tomatoes, peeled, seeded and diced, or 2 x 400 g/14 oz cans chopped tomatoes

1 fresh bay leaf

1 tsp tomato purée

1 tbsp caster sugar

handful roughly chopped fresh herbs, such as flatleaf parsley, marjoram and basil

salt and freshly ground black pepper

This sauce can be adapted by adding a few chillies or some chopped smoked streaky bacon or pancetta. Fresh tomatoes can also be roasted whole until charred and blackened for a more smoky flavour. Alternatively use the canned variety: if you buy a good-quality canned tomato, at least you know it has been sun-ripened and so contains flavour.

1 Heat a pan and add the oil, then stir in the onion, garlic and celery and cook for about 5 minutes until softened but not coloured, stirring occasionally. Pour in the wine and allow to bubble away, then add the tomatoes with the bay leaf, tomato purée and sugar. Season to taste.

2 Bring the sauce to the simmer, then simmer gently for about 30 minutes, stirring occasionally, until the sauce is well reduced and thickened. Remove from the heat and leave to cool a little.

3 When the sauce has cooled, discard the bay leaf and blitz in batches in a food processor until smooth. Pass through a sieve and fold in the herbs. Season to taste and reheat gently to use as required.

84 Watermelon and Grappa Lollies

SERVES 10–12

175g/6 oz caster sugar

finely pared rind of 4 limes, all white pith removed

900 g/2 lb watermelon, cut into chunks and seeds removed

4 tablespoons Grappa

juice of 2 limes

Refreshing and aromatic, these lollies are excellent thirst-quenchers on hot summer days. Adding the lime syrup enhances the watermelon's elusive taste and the Grappa gives the lollies a powerful punch. Pass them around at the end of a barbecue or serve them after a spicy meal to help refresh and clean the palate. I also like to make mango and rum lollies in exactly the same way; or you can omit the alcohol to keep the kids happy.

1 Place the sugar in a pan and pour in 175 ml/6 fl oz water. Place over a very gentle heat and allow the sugar to dissolve, without boiling, until completely clear. Bring the syrup to the boil and boil for 4–5 minutes until it is 102°C/215°F – short thread stage. Remove from the heat and place the pan in a basin filled with cold water to cool the syrup slightly. Stir in the lime rind and allow to chill. You should have 120 ml/4 fl oz of lime sugar syrup in total.

2 Place the watermelon in a food processor and process for 1–2 minutes or until the watermelon has liquefied. Strain through a sieve into a large jug and stir in the lime sugar syrup, Grappa and lime juice. Pour the mixture into 10–12 ice-lolly moulds. Place in the freezer for 4–6 hours or until the lollies are completely frozen. Quickly dip the lolly moulds into hot water to remove the lollies and serve.

85 Tiramisú

SERVES 4

3 egg yolks (preferably free-range or organic)

75 g/3 oz caster sugar

2 x 250 g/9 oz tubs mascarpone cheese

85 ml/3 fl oz Kahlua or coffee liqueur

200 ml/7 fl oz cold strong coffee or espresso

14 boudoir or sponge finger biscuits

25 g/1 oz plain chocolate, finely grated

cocoa powder, for dusting

Mascarpone is a rich, creamy cheese originating in Lodi in the Lombardy region of Italy. It has a sweetened taste and is famously used in Tiramisú, which is basically a cream cheese and rum 'trifle' with hints of coffee and chocolate. To bring this dessert a touch more up to date I like to serve it in individual glass coffee cups set on saucers, but you could always just layer it up in one single glass dish if you prefer. Look out for the Lion Quality Mark when buying eggs as it guarantees quality and freshness.

1 Place the egg yolks in a bowl with the caster sugar and beat together until pale and thickened, using an electric whisk. Add the mascarpone and whisk slowly until the mixture is pale and smooth. Pour in 1 tablespoon of the Kahlua or coffee liqueur and whisk gently to combine.

2 Mix the coffee with the remaining Kahlua or coffee liqueur in a shallow dish. Dip half of the boudoir or sponge finger biscuits into the coffee mixture and arrange in the bottom of four glass coffee cups, breaking them up as necessary. Spoon over half the mascarpone mixture and sprinkle half the chocolate on top. Repeat the layers and then cover each one with cling film. Chill for least for 2 hours (up to 24 hours is fine). Set on saucers and dust with cocoa powder just before serving.

123

86 Bread-and-Butter Pudding

SERVES 6–8

50 g/2 oz sultanas

50 g/2 oz raisins

4 tbsp brandy

14 slices medium-sliced white bread

150 g/5 oz unsalted butter, softened

4 eggs, plus 4 egg yolks (preferably free-range or organic)

100 g/4 oz icing sugar

2 tsp vanilla extract

450 ml/³/₄ pint milk

750 ml/1¹/₂ pints double cream

pinch freshly grated nutmeg

2–3 tbsp caster sugar

apricot compote, (good-quality, shop-bought is fine) to serve

An English classic, but made in so many different ways. Anton Mosimann has probably done more to make this dish famous than any other chef in the last decade; he makes an extremely light 'souffléd' version. I personally prefer the classic soft set with an exquisitely light spicing of cinnamon and nutmeg, a few raisins and sultanas soaked in brandy and a wonderful buttery top. It is also fabulous made with day-old brioches or croissants.

1 Place the sultanas and raisins in a small, non-metallic bowl and pour over the brandy. Cover with cling film and leave to soak for at least 2 hours (overnight is best). Drain off any excess brandy and reserve.

2 Butter the bread using 100 g/4 oz of the butter. Remove the crusts and cut each slice into four triangles. Grease a 2.25-litre/4-pint, shallow, ovenproof dish with a little of the remaining butter and arrange a layer of the bread triangles in the bottom of the dish, buttered-side up. Scatter over half of the soaked dried fruit and place another layer of the bread triangles on top, buttered-side up – you should have used about two-thirds of them at this stage. Set the remainder of the bread triangles aside. Scatter over the remaining soaked dried fruit and press down gently with a fish slice.

3 To make the custard, whisk together the eggs, egg yolks and icing sugar in a large jug. Add the vanilla extract, milk and double cream, whisking to combine. Pour two-thirds of the custard over the layered-up bread triangles and leave to stand for 45 minutes–1 hour until the bread has soaked up all of the custard. Pour the reserved brandy into the rest of the custard and set aside.

4 Preheat the oven to 180°C/350°F/Gas 4; fan oven 160°C from cold. Pour the brandy-and-custard mixture over the soaked bread-and-butter triangles. Arrange the reserved bread triangles on top, buttered-side up. Press the slices down firmly with a fish slice so that the custard comes halfway up the bread triangles. Sprinkle over the nutmeg and caster sugar, then dot with the remaining butter. Place the dish into a roasting tin and fill with warm water so that it comes three-quarters of the way up the dish. Bake for 35–40 minutes or until the custard has just set and the top is golden brown. Serve, cut into slices, with the apricot compote.

87 Twice-baked Chocolate Soufflés

SERVES 4

100 g/4 oz plain chocolate (70 per cent cocoa solids)

225 ml/8 fl oz milk

50 g/2 oz unsalted butter, plus extra for greasing

4 tbsp plain flour

4 large eggs (preferably free-range or organic), separated

5 tbsp caster sugar, plus extra for dusting

2 tbsp cocoa powder, sifted

300 ml/^{1}/$_2$ pint double cream

icing sugar, for dusting

crème fraîche, to serve

There is something about chocolate that is addictive. It contains several stimulants, including caffeine and pleasure-inducing endorphins! These are intensely chocolaty soufflés that get baked twice. They really couldn't be simpler to make and you don't have any last-minute worries about whether they're going to rise.

1 Preheat the oven to 190°C/375°F/Gas 5; fan oven 170°C from cold. Melt the chocolate in a heatproof bowl set over a pan of simmering water. Heat the milk in a pan until just at boiling point. Remove the milk from the heat and stir in half the melted chocolate. Melt the butter in a small pan, stir in the flour and cook over a low heat for 1 minute. Remove from the heat and gradually add the milk, stirring until smooth after each addition. Return to the heat and cook for a few minutes, stirring until smooth and shiny. Transfer to a large bowl with a spatula; leave to cool a little.

2 Add the egg yolks one at a time, mixing well into the chocolate sauce, then remove 2 tablespoons and set aside. Using an electric beater, whisk the egg whites in a bowl until soft peaks form. Add 3 tablespoons of the caster sugar and whisk again for 30 seconds, then fold in 1 tablespoon of the cocoa powder. Lightly beat a third of the egg whites into the chocolate mixture until blended. Add the rest of the egg whites and gently fold in. Divide between four 250-ml/8-fl oz buttered and sugared ramekins. Place on a baking sheet and bake for 15–20 minutes until the soufflés are well risen and a light crust has formed.

3 Place the cream in a small pan with the remaining caster sugar and melted chocolate and whisk in the reserved 2 tablespoons chocolate sauce. Mix the remaining cocoa powder with a little water to make a paste and stir into the pan. Simmer for a few minutes. Remove the soufflés from the oven and quickly tip them out of the ramekins into an ovenproof dish, right-side up. Pour over the chocolate sauce and bake for 10–15 minutes until the soufflés have risen and the sauce is bubbling. Transfer the soufflés to serving plates, stir the sauce and spoon around them. Dust with icing sugar and a quenelle of crème fraîche to serve.

88 Raspberry-ripple Zabaglione

SERVES 4

225 g/8 oz fresh raspberries

1/2 lemon, pips removed

icing sugar, to taste, plus extra for dusting

4 egg yolks (preferably free-range or organic)

2 tbsp caster sugar

2 tbsp medium-dry sherry

2 tbsp dry white wine

4 tbsp double cream

crisp wafer-thin biscuits, to serve

This classic Italian pud is traditionally made with eggs, sugar and Marsala in the same way as sabayon, beaten over simmering water until a thick froth is produced. It can be eaten warm or cold, and of course there are many variations, of which this is one. You can use any soft fruit that is in season, or a good store-cupboard standby would be a can of apricots in natural juice, just drained and blitzed to a purée.

1 Place the raspberries in a food processor (reserving twelve for decoration) with a good squeeze of lemon juice. Blitz to a purée, then push through a nylon sieve to remove the seeds. Add icing sugar to taste, leaving it slightly on the tart side, then set aside.

2 Place the egg yolks and caster sugar in a large, heatproof bowl. Beat in the sherry and wine, using a balloon whisk. Place over a pan of simmering water and heat gently, whisking continuously, until the mixture is very light but can hold its shape. When it is the consistency of semi-melted ice-cream, take it off the heat and continue to whisk over a bowl of iced water until cool – this prevents it from 'splitting'.

3 Whip the cream in a bowl until it just holds its shape, then fold into the zabaglione mixture. Drizzle in the raspberry purée and gently swirl in to give a ripple effect. Spoon into stemmed serving glasses and serve at once, decorated with the reserved raspberries and a dusting of icing sugar, with crisp biscuits on the side; or chill until ready to serve.

89 Rhubarb Crumble

No. 4 CLASSIC DISHES

SERVES 6-8

1 kg/2¼ lb forced rhubarb, cut into 4-cm /1½ in-pieces

175 g/6 oz caster sugar

grated rind and juice of 1 orange

juice of 1 lemon

2.5-cm/1-in piece fresh root ginger, peeled and grated

FOR THE TOPPING:

25 g/1 oz powdered milk

25 g/1 oz ground almonds

25 g/1 oz rolled oats

225 g/8 oz plain flour

250 g/8 oz dark muscovado sugar

1 tsp ground cinnamon

½ tsp salt

175 g/6 oz unsalted butter, chilled and cut into cubes

clotted cream, to serve

A classic combination of rhubarb with a crumble topping. I just love making this with Champagne rhubarb, the sweetest of all. It arrives very early in spring and has slim, tender stalks. However, the rhubarb can be replaced with plums or a mixture of blackberry and apple if you'd prefer. The crumble mixture really works well on top of any fruit and the dark muscovado sugar gives the crumble its classic crunchiness. My secret ingredient is milk powder, which blends with the juices of the rhubarb to help make the most delicious sauce.

1 Preheat the oven to 180°C/350°F/Gas 4; fan oven 160°C from cold. Tip the rhubarb into an ovenproof dish and sprinkle over the caster sugar, orange rind and juice, lemon juice, ginger and 2 tablespoons water. Stir gently to mix and set aside.

2 To make the topping, place the powdered milk, ground almonds, oats, flour, sugar, cinnamon and salt in a food processor and pulse together briefly just to combine. Add the butter and continue to pulse until the mixture resembles a crumble. Scatter over the top of the rhubarb mixture and bake for 45 minutes–1 hour or until the top is golden brown and the edges are bubbling up. Serve hot or cold in serving bowls with clotted cream.

90 Baked Bramleys

SERVES 4

4 Bramley cooking apples, each about 300 g/11 oz

50 g/2 oz unsalted butter

50 g/2 oz ready-to-eat dried apricots, finely diced

4 generous tbsp clear honey

40 g/1¹/₂ oz toasted flaked almonds

large fresh mint sprigs and icing sugar, to decorate

custard (see p. 132), to serve

This recipe brings back memories of childhood, although it is a little more sophisticated than the baked apples I enjoyed then. Baked apples always seem to be popular, especially served with homemade custard. There are numerous variations when it comes to stuffing Bramleys; however, I have to say that this one works particularly well. If you want to ring the changes, substitute the apricots with raisins, sultanas or even dates, or try a mixture. Sweet mincemeat also works a treat nearer to Christmas.

1 Preheat the oven to 180°C/350°F/Gas 4; fan oven 160°C from cold. Remove the core and a little bit more from each apple and then run the tip of a sharp knife around the circumference of each one, just piercing the skin – this helps to stop them bursting while cooking. Use 40 g/1¹/₂ oz of the butter to grease a 23-cm/9-in square ovenproof dish that will fit the apples comfortably. Arrange the apples in the dish.

2 Place the apricots in a bowl with the honey and almonds and stir to combine, then divide between the cavities of the apples and pile up the excess in a dome on top of the fruit. Dot with the remaining butter and bake for 45 minutes–1 hour, basting every 10–15 minutes, until the apples are completely tender but still holding their shape. Cover the tops of the apples with small pieces of foil if they start to brown too quickly.

3 Transfer the apples to wide-rimmed serving bowls set on plates and spoon around the custard. Decorate with large mint sprigs to look like stalks and add a good dusting of icing sugar before serving.

91 Tarte Tatin

SERVES 6

225g/8 oz ready-made puff pastry, thawed if frozen

plain flour, for dusting

6–7 crisp eating apples, such as Egremont Russet or Granny Smith, about 1 kg/2^1/$_4$ lb in total

grated rind and juice of 1 large lemon

100 g/4 oz unsalted butter, at room temperature

175 g/6 oz caster sugar

good pinch freshly grated nutmeg

clotted cream, to serve

The best way to arrange the apples in the tin is to start at the perimeter, in a pinwheel fashion, filling the middle after a full circle of halves is in place. It is very important that they are tightly packed or they are in danger of falling over in the cooking process. If you want to ring the changes, try using pineapple slices or pear halves. The tart can also be reheated in the oven for about 15 minutes if you'd prefer to serve it warm.

1 Roll out the pastry on a lightly floured surface to a round 2.5 cm/1 in larger than a 23–25-cm/9–10-in heavy-based ovenproof frying pan, tarte Tatin mould or shallow cake tin (not a loose-based one) that is about 3 mm/^{1}/$_8$ in thick (but no thicker than 5 mm/^{1}/$_4$ in or it will not cook properly). Place the pastry on a baking sheet lined with non-stick baking paper and chill for at least 30 minutes.

2 Preheat the oven to 200°C/400°F/Gas 6; fan oven 180°C from cold. Peel, core and halve the apples and toss them in half of the lemon juice. Using a spatula, spread the butter evenly into the frying pan, tarte Tatin mould or cake tin. Sprinkle over the sugar in an even layer and arrange the apple halves, cut-side up, tightly together in the bottom of the pan. Cook over a high heat for about 15 minutes or until the apples are caramelized and light golden brown. Remove from the heat, then sprinkle the apples with the nutmeg, lemon rind and the remaining lemon juice. Leave to cool a little, if time allows.

3 Lay the chilled pastry sheet over the top of the apples, tucking in the edges and turning them down so that when the tart is turned out, the edges will create a rim that will hold in the caramel and apple juices. Bake for 25–30 minutes until the pastry is golden brown and the apples are completely tender but still holding their shape.

4 Leave the tart in the tin for a minute or two, then loosen the edges with a round-bladed knife and invert on to a flat serving plate. Rearrange any apples that have loosened back into place with a palette knife and leave to cool, if time allows. This enables all the juices to be reabsorbed and allows the caramel to set slightly because of the pectin in the apples. Cut into slices and serve on slightly warmed plates with lashings of clotted cream.

92 Treacle Sponge

No. 8 BEST OF BRITISH

SERVES 6–8

3 tbsp golden syrup
1 tbsp fresh white bread-crumbs

juice of $1/2$ lemon

175 g/6 oz unsalted butter, softened, plus extra for greasing

175 g/6 oz caster sugar

grated rind of 1 lemon

3 eggs (preferably free-range or organic), beaten

200 g/7 oz self-raising flour

about 3 tbsp milk

FOR THE CUSTARD:

300 ml/$1/2$ pint milk

450 ml/$3/4$ pint double cream

1 vanilla pod, split in half and seeds scraped out

6 egg yolks (preferably free-range or organic)

4 tbsp caster sugar

Steamed puddings are excellent fodder and I'm sure on most people's list of favourite nursery foods. If you're short of time, you can microwave the pud in just a few minutes, although you won't get quite the same depth of flavour.

1 Place the golden syrup in a small bowl with the breadcrumbs and lemon juice and mix well to combine. Grease a 1.2-litre/2-pint pudding basin with a little butter and then pour the golden syrup mixture into the bottom and set aside.

2 To make the sponge, place the butter and sugar in a bowl and gently cream together, using an electric whisk. Mix in the lemon rind and then slowly whisk in the eggs, a little at a time. Sift in the flour and gently whisk to combine. Fold in just enough milk for the mixture to drop easily from the spoon.

3 Spoon the sponge mixture into the pudding basin and cover with a circle of greaseproof paper, then place a double piece of buttered foil on top, pleated in the centre to allow room for expansion while cooking. Secure with string, making a handle so that you can easily lift it out of the hot steamer. Place the pudding on an upturned plate inside a large pan and pour in enough boiling water to come two-thirds up the sides of the basin. Steam for $1^{3}/_{4}$–2 hours, topping up with boiling water occasionally so as to prevent the pan from boiling dry.

4 Meanwhile, make the custard. Pour the milk into a small pan and add the cream and scraped-out vanilla seeds. Place over a gentle heat and slowly bring to the boil. Place the egg yolks and sugar in a bowl and beat together until well combined, using a wooden spoon. Remove the milk mixture from the heat and slowly whisk it into the egg mixture. Pour back into the pan and place on a gentle heat. Cook, without allowing to boil, until the custard coats the back of a wooden spoon, stirring continuously. If the custard becomes lumpy, simply sieve it into a large warmed jug, then cover with cling film to prevent a skin forming.

5 Remove the pudding basin from the pan and allow to cool slightly. Place the custard in a small pan or in the microwave to reheat gently, if liked. Cut away the string from the pudding basin and remove the foil and greaseproof paper. Invert the treacle sponge on to a serving plate, ensuring that all the syrup has come out from the bottom of the basin. Cut into wedges and serve with plenty of custard.

93 Tropical Fruit Pavlova

SERVES 6–8

4 large egg whites (preferably free-range or organic), at room temperature

pinch salt

225 g/8 oz caster sugar

2 tsp cornflour

pinch cream of tartar

1 tsp white wine vinegar

4 drops vanilla extract

2 passion fruit

selection ripe tropical fruit, such as mango, kiwi, star fruit and cape gooseberries

150 ml/¹/₄ pint double cream

200 ml/7 fl oz crème fraîche

I wonder sometimes whether the invention of Pavlova was a mistake – a meringue gone wrong – but it's very popular and goes down a treat with me. Unlike genuine meringues, the intention is to have a crisp shell with a gooey, toffee-ish centre. This is achieved by adding a touch of cornflour and vinegar to the meringue. The cooked 'Pav' should have a pinky hue to it, but shouldn't go brown. Use any fruit you like to decorate, but I think that a tropical selection works particularly well with the sweetness of the pavlova.

1 Preheat the oven to 150°C/300°F/Gas 2; fan oven 130°C from cold. Line a baking sheet with non-stick baking paper and draw on a 20-cm/8-in circle. To make the meringue, whisk the egg whites and salt in a large, clean bowl until stiff peaks have formed. Whisk in the sugar a third at a time, whisking well between each addition until stiff and very shiny. Sprinkle over the cornflour, cream of tartar, vinegar and vanilla extract and fold in gently.

2 Pile the meringue on to the paper within the circle, making sure there is a sub-stantial hollow in the centre. Place in the oven and immediately reduce the heat to 120°C/250°F/Gas ¹/₂; fan oven 100°C and continue to cook for 1¹/₂–2 hours until crisp but still a little soft in the centre. Turn off the oven, leave the door slightly ajar and leave to cool completely.

3 To make the filling, halve the passion fruit and scoop out the pulp. Peel and slice your selection of fruit as necessary. Place the cream in a bowl and whip until thickened, then fold in the crème fraîche. Peel the paper off the pavlova and place on a plate. Pile on the cream mixture and arrange the fruit on top, finishing with the passion-fruit pulp. Cut into slices and arrange on plates to serve.

94　Sticky Toffee Pudding

SERVES 6–8

175 g/6 oz unsalted butter, softened, plus extra for greasing

175 g/6 oz dates (preferably Medjool), stoned and chopped

1 tsp bicarbonate of soda

175 g/6 oz golden caster sugar

1 tsp vanilla extract

2 eggs (preferably free-range or organic), beaten

175 g/6 oz self-raising flour, sifted

100 g/4 oz dark muscovado sugar

4 tbsp clear honey or golden syrup

4 tbsp double cream

vanilla ice-cream, to serve

I normally make one big pudding, but you can also make small individual ones. This quantity will fill eight 150-ml/¼-pint greased dariole moulds – you might want to put a circle of non-stick baking paper in the bottom of each one so that the puddings turn out easily. Arrange them in a bain marie (a roasting tin half-filled with boiling water) and bake for 25–30 minutes or until well risen.

1 Preheat the oven to 180°C/350°F/Gas 4; fan oven 160°C from cold. Grease a 25 x 18-cm/10 x 7-in non-stick baking tin that is at least 2.5 cm/1 in deep. Place the dates in a pan with 300 ml/½ pint water and bring to the boil, then simmer for 5 minutes until softened. Remove from the heat and stir in the bicarbonate of soda until the mixture stops foaming.

2 Place 50 g/2 oz of the butter and the caster sugar in a large bowl and cream together until light and fluffy, using an electric mixer, then beat in the vanilla. Gradually add the eggs, beating well after each addition. Fold in the flour with a metal spoon and finally fold in the date mixture. Pour into the greased baking tin and bake for about 35–40 minutes until well risen and firm to the touch.

3 To make the toffee sauce, simply place the remaining butter, the muscovado sugar and honey or golden syrup in a pan and heat gently, stirring until the sugar has dissolved. Bring to a simmer and cook for 2–3 minutes until thickened. Stir in the cream and allow to bubble down, then remove from the heat.

4 When the pudding is cooked, remove from the oven and after 5 minutes turn out on to a wire rack to cool completely. To serve, cut the pudding into portions and arrange on plates. Pour over some of the toffee sauce, then flash under a hot grill until bubbling, if liked. Add a scoop of ice-cream and serve the remainder of the sauce separately, hot or cold.

95 Banana Flambée

SERVES 2-4

40 g/1¹/₂ oz unsalted butter

4 large bananas, cut into 3 even-sized slices on the diagonal

¹/₄ tsp ground allspice

50 g/2 oz light muscovado sugar

juice of 1 lime

4 tbsp light rum

vanilla ice cream, to serve (optional)

During the 1980s whenever I was in New York I always loved eating Häagen Dazs' ice creams, and then they came over here. Ice cream is sexy food and with hot banana and the toffee-like sauce this is a very sexy dish. I always get rave reviews when I serve it – bananas in all guises are one of my weaknesses...

1 Heat a large, heavy-based pan or wok. Melt the butter and add the bananas. Cook over a fairly high heat, tossing constantly, until lightly golden, then sprinkle over the allspice and sugar. Continue to cook for another minute or so until the bananas have just begun to caramelize, tossing occasionally.

2 Pour the lime juice into the pan with half of the rum and simmer for another 2–3 minutes or until the bananas are completely tender but still holding their shape. Heat the remaining rum in a small pan. Bring the bananas to the table, if liked, then pour over the heated rum and set alight. Allow the flames to die down, spoon into wide-rimmed bowls and serve with a scoop of ice-cream, if liked.

96 Rum Fruit 'n' Nut Truffles

SERVES 6–8

50 g/2 oz sultanas, chopped

2 tbsp dark rum

75 g/3 oz walnuts, finely chopped

225 g/8 oz plain cooking chocolate

25 g/1 oz unsalted butter, cut into small pieces

1 large egg yolk (preferably free-range or organic)

50 ml/2 fl oz double cream

50 g/2 oz dates (preferably Medjool), chopped

You can use a number of different coatings for these truffles depending on what takes your fancy. Try melted plain or white chocolate, cocoa powder, finely grated chocolate or finely chopped toasted almonds. If you decide to use melted or finely grated chocolate, you'll need an extra 175 g/6 oz. Make sure you use good-quality cooking chocolate or they are really not worth making: I find Green & Black's, with 70 per cent cocoa solids, the best.

1 Place the sultanas in a small bowl with the rum and set aside to soak for at least 2 hours (overnight is best). Place the walnuts in a heavy-based frying pan and lightly toast, tossing occasionally. Remove from the heat and leave to cool.

2 Break the chocolate into a heatproof bowl and melt over a pan of simmering water or in the microwave on high for 2–3 minutes. Stir the chocolate until it has completely melted, then add the butter and continue to stir until melted. Leave to cool a little.

3 Add the egg yolk to the chocolate mixture with the cream, dates and soaked sultana mixture, then beat with a wooden spoon for 5 minutes until well combined. Cover the bowl with plastic film and chill for at least 2 hours (up to 24 hours is fine) to allow the mixture to firm up.

4 Using a Parisienne scoop or melon baller, scoop out balls of the truffle mixture and roll in the toasted walnuts or another coating of your choice. Place the truffles in mini muffin cups or sweet paper cases – you should have 24 in total. Store in an airtight container in the fridge and they will happily keep for up to 2 weeks until you are ready to serve.

97 Apple Tart with a Twist

No. 2 CLASSIC DISHES

SERVES 6–8

8 Bramley cooking apples, about 1.25 kg/2¹/₂ lb in total

juice of 1 lemon

50 g/2 oz unsalted butter

50g/2 oz caster sugar

450 g/1 lb ready-made rolled puff pastry, thawed if frozen

flour, for dusting

beaten egg, to glaze

1–2 tbsp icing sugar

Calvados custard, to serve

This tart is really simple. Prepare with good old Bramley apples, pop in the oven for 20 minutes and voilà – apple tart! Serve with some Calvados custard, which can be easily made by stirring 2 tablespoons of Calvados into a carton of ready-made custard. Alternatively you can heat a ladleful of Calvados over the gas flame of a hob until it burns, then drizzle over the apple tart – delicious. To make your life much easier use a packet of ready-rolled puff pastry sheets for this tart.

1 Peel and core the apples and cut each one in half, then place in a bowl with the lemon juice and pour in enough water to cover. Melt half of the butter in a pan and add half of the apples, cover and simmer gently for 20 minutes, stirring occasionally. Remove the lid and beat in the caster sugar until you have achieved a smooth purée. Take off the heat and leave to cool completely.

2 Roll the pastry a little thinner on a lightly floured work surface, then trim down the edges. Transfer to a baking sheet lined with non-stick baking paper and chill for at least 30 minutes.

3 Preheat the oven to 200°C/400°F/Gas 6; fan oven 180°C from cold. Remove the pastry from the fridge and spread the purée over the pastry base using a spatula, leaving a 1-cm/¹/₂-in border around the edges. Drain the remaining apple halves and cut them into thin slices, then use them to cover the apple purée in an over-lapping layer. Brush the border with the beaten egg and dot the apple slices with the remaining butter. Bake for 15–20 minutes until the pastry is puffed up and golden brown and the apple slices are tender and lightly golden.

4 Remove the tart from the oven and sprinkle over enough icing sugar to cover the apple slices, then use a blow-torch to caramelize the apples (alternatively you could place the tart under a very hot grill for a few seconds). Cut the tart into slices and place on serving plates, then spoon over a little of the custard to serve.

98 Lime Sorbet with Griddled Mango

SERVES 4

3 limes

250 g/9 oz golden caster sugar, plus 1 tbsp

10 good-quality tea bags (Orange Pekoe Ceylon work particularly well)

2 large, ripe, firm mangoes, peeled and cut into 1-cm/ $^1/_2$ in slices

Juicy limes are very important for this dessert. Thin-skinned limes yield the most juice, as do slightly older ones, recognized by their muddy yellow colour. So it's often worth popping down to the market and seeking out older stock – at a knocked-down price of course!

1 Pare the rind from the limes and chop into tiny pieces. Place in a small pan and cover with water. Bring to the boil to blanch, then tip into a fine sieve and refresh under cold running water.

2 To make the syrup, place the sugar in a pan with 1 litre/1$^3/_4$ pints water and cook over a low heat until dissolved, then boil fast for 2–3 minutes. Remove from the heat, pour into a large bowl and set aside, leaving 150 ml/$^1/_4$ pint of the syrup behind in the pan. Add the blanched lime rind to the pan and simmer for about 15 minutes until completely tender, stirring occasionally and being careful not to let it boil away and burn.

3 Place 300 ml/$^1/_2$ pint water in a separate pan with the tea bags and bring to the boil, then remove from the heat and set aside for 3–5 minutes to infuse. Taste after 3 minutes: if you are happy with the flavour, remove the tea bags; if you want it a little stronger, infuse with the tea bags for a few more minutes – just don't allow the tea to infuse for too long or it will become bitter. Strain into a jug, discarding the tea bags.

4 Cut the limes in half, and squeeze the juice through a fine strainer into a bowl, then stir into the reserved sugar syrup. Add the rind mixture and the tea infusion and stir to combine. It is important to taste at this stage – you may want to add extra sugar or lime juice accordingly – then leave to cool completely. Place into an ice-cream/sorbet machine and churn according to the manufacturer's instructions. You should get 1.2 litres/2 pints of sorbet in total.

5 When you are ready to serve, heat a very clean griddle pan. Lightly sprinkle one side of each mango slice with half of the remaining tablespoon of sugar. Place on the heated griddle pan, sugar-side down – you'll probably have to do this in batches – and cook for 2–3 minutes. Sprinkle the rest of the sugar over the mango slices, turn them over and cook on the other side for another 2–3 minutes or until the mango is lightly charred and caramelized. Arrange on plates and serve hot with scoops of the lime sorbet.

99 Lemon Polenta Cake with Rosemary Syrup

SERVES 8–10

175 g/6 oz polenta (fine cornmeal)

50 g/2 oz plain flour

1¹/₂ tsp baking powder

¹/₄ tsp salt

5 tbsp plain yoghurt

5 tbsp rapeseed or sunflower oil, plus extra for greasing

grated rind of 2 lemons

2 tbsp lemon juice

2 eggs, plus 2 egg whites (preferably free-range or organic)

400 g/14 oz caster sugar

2 branches fresh rosemary, plus extra sprigs to decorate

fresh raspberries and Greek yoghurt, to serve

They don't come much simpler than this unusual cake, which originates from Italy. Its crumb is textured and scented. Its beauty lies in its lack of adornment – just a drizzle of the rosemary syrup and a few raspberries and a dollop of Greek yoghurt. Yet, for all its plainness, it has flavour that money can't buy. It also keeps really well in an airtight container for up to a week, the rosemary syrup helping it to stay moist. For a completely different result replace the lemons with oranges or limes; or use a mixture of citrus fruit.

1 Preheat the oven to 180°C/350°F/Gas 4; fan oven 160°C from cold. Sift the polenta, flour, baking powder and salt into a bowl. Place the yoghurt, oil, lemon rind and juice into a jug and stir until combined.

2 In a separate bowl, beat the eggs and egg whites with half of the sugar for a few minutes until creamy. Beat in the yoghurt mixture until smooth and then fold in the dry ingredients until just combined – do not over-mix.

3 Pour the batter mixture into a 1.2-litre/2-pint lightly oiled loaf tin lined with greaseproof paper. Bake for 40–45 minutes until a thin skewer inserted in the centre comes out clean.

4 Meanwhile, place the remaining sugar in a pan with 200 ml/7 fl oz water and the rosemary branches. Bring to the boil, reduce the heat and simmer for 10 minutes. Leave to cool completely, then strain through a sieve.

5 When the cake is cooked, place on a wire rack to cool for 15 minutes, then invert and peel off the greaseproof paper. Prick all over with a thin skewer or toothpick and drizzle over half of the rosemary syrup so that it completely soaks into the cake. Leave to cool completely. Keep the remaining rosemary syrup in the fridge until ready to use.

6 To serve, cut the cake into slices and arrange on plates. Scatter around the raspberries and drizzle around some more of the syrup. Add dollops of the Greek yoghurt and decorate with rosemary sprigs.

100 Glazed Lemon Tart

SERVES 6-8

175 g/6 oz unsalted butter, diced

25 g/1 oz icing sugar, sifted, plus extra for dusting

pinch salt

7 eggs, plus 1 egg yolk (preferably free-range or organic)

juice and finely grated rind of 3 lemons (preferably unwaxed)

50 g/2 oz toasted almonds, finely ground

225 g/8 oz plain flour, sifted, plus extra for dusting

300 g/11 oz caster sugar

300 ml/¹/₂ pint double cream

crème fraîche, to serve

This classic lemon tart was first popularized by the Roux brothers and subsequently by Marco Pierre White. Whenever I put it on the menu, it outsells all other puddings. As a variation on the normal shortbread tart base, I add some ground toasted almonds and grated lemon rind. Try to leave the filling in the fridge for the full 2 days to allow the flavours to develop. If you really want to show off, glaze the top of the tart with sugar.

1 Place the butter in a food processor with the icing sugar, salt, one of the eggs and 1 dessertspoon of the lemon rind and blend for 20 seconds. Add the ground almonds and flour and blend until the dough just comes together. Place in a polythene bag and chill for at least 2 hours.

2 Beat 6 eggs and the caster sugar in a bowl until well blended, using a wooden spoon. Stir in the cream and then the rest of the lemon rind and all of the juice. Pour into a jug (it should make 1 litre/1³/₄ pints), cover with cling film and chill for at least 2 hours (up to 2 days is best).

3 Preheat the oven to 180°C/350°F/Gas 5; fan oven 160°C from cold. Take the pastry out of the fridge and coarsely break into a 23-cm/9-in loose-bottomed flan tin that is 2.5 cm/1 in deep. Quickly press the pastry up the sides and into the shape of the tin. Keep or discard any excess pastry.

4 Lightly prick the base with a fork in several places. Line the pastry with a circle of greaseproof paper and fill with ceramic baking beans. Chill for 20 minutes, then bake blind for 12 minutes. Remove from the oven and take out the beans and paper. Beat the egg yolk and use to brush the base, then bake for another 8 minutes until lightly golden and 'glazed'.

5 Reduce the oven temperature to 150°C/300°F/Gas 2; fan oven 130°C. Give the lemon filling a good stir, pour into the glazed pastry crust and bake for 35–45 minutes until just set with no wobble in the middle. Allow to cool, then carefully lift out of the flan tin. Score the tart into portions and, using a tea strainer as a sieve, dust with icing sugar. Glaze with a blow-torch or under a hot grill. Cut into slices and arrange on plates with some crème fraîche to serve.

Index